A Wholesome Horror

Poor Houses in Nova Scotia

BRENDA THOMPSON

SSP Publications

© 2017 Brenda Thompson

SSP Publications recognizes the support of the Province of Nova Scotia. We are pleased to work in partnership with the Department of Communities, Culture and Heritage to develop and promote our cultural resources for all Nova Scotians.

NOVA SCOTIA

Front cover image: Lance Woolaver
Back cover image: Steven Rhude painting, photo by Ernest Cadegan
Design: Gwen North

Library and Archives Canada Cataloguing in Publication

Thompson, Brenda, 1963-, author
   A wholesome horror : poor houses in Nova Scotia / Brenda Thompson.

Includes bibliographical references and index.
ISBN 978-0-9868733-5-5 (softcover)

   1. Almshouses--Nova Scotia--History. 2. Public welfare--Nova Scotia-- History. 3. Poor laws--Nova Scotia--History. I. Title.

HV63.C3T46 2018   362.5'8309716   C2018-901359-1

Publications

Box 2472, Halifax, N.S. B3J 3E4 Canada
sspub.ca
sspub@hotmail.com

Printed in Canada

For My Parents,
Juanita and Richard Thompson

Acknowledgements

Without the love and support of my family, I would never have been able to reach my writing goals. Thank you to my daughters, Megan and Gwynneth Thompson, who put up with me constantly shushing and ignoring them so that I could write; to my parents, Rick and Juanita Thompson, who read over every word and encouraged me to write more; and to my husband, Kent Folks, who tolerated my papers and books everywhere and listened to single topic conversations for months.

To Scott Smith, thank you for encouraging me to write and for publishing this book. We had great conversations! Let's do it again!

Thank you to Wayne E. Baltzer for enthusiastically sharing his private collection of photos and research about poor houses in Kings County.

To Lance Woolaver, who had encouraged me to write and regularly checks in to see how my writing is going.

A special shout-out to the Halifax-based writing group called Senior Scribes and Dr. Allan Marble, who wrote about the most unpopular of subjects – poor people. They examined the lives of poor people with open minds when most writers dismissed people living in poverty as victims of their own bad decisions.

And finally, thanks to all of those who have lived in poverty or are now living in poverty and still fight to survive and make life better for themselves, their families and other poor people – despite being up against powerful adversaries who wish to keep them where they are.

Contents

Foreword

One of the great pleasures in a writing life is the meeting up with other writers. I greatly enjoyed meeting Brenda Thompson in the summer of 2017, together with her partner Kent Folks, at our home in Halifax, not remembering that we had met in Annapolis Royal years ago at the first production of *Maud Lewis: World Without Shadows* at King's Theatre in Annapolis Royal. Fortunately, Brenda's memory is much better than mine. She works harder too.

I was intrigued by the prospect of Brenda's new book. The poor houses and poor farms of Nova Scotia were subjects in which I have long been interested. This interest grew out of my books and plays and film about Maud Lewis, the Nova Scotia folk artist. I knew that Maud had avoided incarceration in a poor house in Yarmouth County, Nova Scotia following the birth of her out-of-wedlock child in 1928. And I knew that Maud had become friends with the kindly and charitable Olive Hayden, Matron of the Almshouse (see definition p. 56) of the Poor Farm in Marshalltown, Digby County, following Olive's marriage to the Keeper, Halton Hayden, in 1939. Maud and her husband, the poor farm night watchman Everett Lewis, were welcome to take their meals at the Almshouse. And I had written a play set in the old Marshalltown Almshouse entitled *The Poor Farm* based on local interviews and village stories. Brenda Thompson, however, has taken this work far beyond my gatherings and presented us with the first comprehensive and complete Nova Scotian account of these houses of poverty: *A Wholesome Horror*. I am happy to have met Brenda again and happy to meet up with her work.

As it turns out, Brenda and I nearly met again in 1995. I was in Digby County in the 1990's and spending a lot of time in and about the still-standing Almshouse and shooting a documentary film. I found myself in Marshalltown the day before the Almshouse burnt down in its fields by the highway; I took the last portrait of this prison for the poor – my partner Bob Brooks, the famous photographer, was on his way from Halifax. Bob arrived after the structure was completely incinerated and took some photos of the smoking ruins. Brenda was among those who gathered during the fire. I missed the fire. The conflagration was adjudged arson, and with the murder of the husband of Maud Lewis, Everett

Lewis, the former child inmate of the Poor Farm, it was the second great crime on that stretch of that country road. Brenda was there for that historic and somehow symbolic moment, just as she presents us now with her original and thorough and very readable history of a story many have preferred to ignore.

There is much in *A Wholesome Horror* that will be new and unknown to Nova Scotians. I did not know that the incarceration of First Nations citizens of Canada in the poor farms was so extensive. I did not know much about the casual and callous use of the unclaimed bodies of poor farm and poor house inmates. I simply did not know the extent of these prisons throughout our idyllic and kind province. We built them and filled them in every county, sometimes two. We incarcerated the unmarried, the elderly, our veterans from foreign wars, unwanted family, the ill, and in bizarre fashion "stubborn children, beggars and fortune tellers," to quote from Brenda's book. And many of these inmates died in these prisons – from fire, from epidemic, from age and neglect. In brief, we were cruel. Our past tells us that every time we built a "charitable" institution in Nova Scotia, we created greater crimes. The few good and kind Keepers and Matrons of the Poor Farms tell us only that a better kind of place was always possible. We were rarely up to the job. The closing of the poor farms and poor houses in the 1960's must have been accompanied by a province-wide whistling past the graveyards.

And now that this story has been told, it is time to support the groups of local people in their own Nova Scotian communities who now attempt to locate and protect the graves where these unrecognized dead lie buried. This too is recounted in Brenda's history. The last indignity of the poor farms and the poor houses was the unmarked burial of the unwanted poor. Local groups of Nova Scotians in their own villages and towns now attempt to right this wrong. It seems so little, the remembrance of these for long years wastelands, but in many cases it has been a struggle. Hopefully, and with the help of Brenda Thompson's work, this struggle can be won. Good job, Brenda.

Lance Woolaver
Nova Scotia
2018

Preface

The title of this book comes from beliefs expressed by Jeremy Bentham (1748–1832), an English philosopher and social reformer. Bentham was born near London to a wealthy family that supported the Conservative Party. He completed his education in elite schools for sons of wealthy families. Despite his upbringing, Bentham was ahead of his time; he advocated individual and economic freedom, freedom of expression, equal rights for women, the separation of church and state, the right to divorce and the decriminalization of homosexual acts. He called for the abolition of slavery, the death penalty and physical punishment, including that of children.

When it came to people living in poverty, however, Bentham espoused ideas that clearly illustrate that he had never experienced poverty or even considered the effects of poverty on people. Instead, he believed that people would do, naturally, whatever was easiest to accomplish their goals. He reasoned that if workers were given the choice between working for their living or going into a poor house, they would choose the latter. Thus, Bentham argued, poor houses must not give comfort to workers but should provide only the meanest basics for living. He also advocated that a stigma be attached to anyone who had lived in a poor house. Bentham proposed that a poor house must be made into "An Object of Wholesome Horror" for workers so that they would keep doing their jobs no matter how demeaning, degrading, or dangerous. Unfortunately, his ideas continue to have a horrendous impact on people living in poverty.

Introduction

"Overcoming poverty is not a gesture of charity. It is the protection of a fundamental human right, the right to dignity and a decent life."
— Nelson Mandela, Former President of South Africa

In March 1993, I was an unwed mother on social assistance (marital status was relevant for social assistance benefits in those days), on my way to Yarmouth for a job interview. I had lived on social assistance with my nine-year-old daughter for the previous seven years and had been embroiled in high profile anti-poverty battles to improve the system. With my newly acquired university degrees and a published book about low income single moms, I was off to try to win my first job as a graduate.

Driving down Highway 101 past Digby, I saw an interesting looking building, which I glanced at several times, wondering what it was. On the way back from the interview, I pulled over to take a look. It was a weatherbeaten, boarded-up structure that looked like a creepy old mansion. It fascinated me.

A few months later, after I had secured the job in Yarmouth, I asked around about the building and found out it had been a poor house, officially called the Marshalltown Almshouse. Like most people, I had heard the expression "putting us in the poor house" and I knew about almshouses in England (see definition p. 56) from books like *Oliver Twist*, but I did not know that there had ever been poor houses in Nova Scotia. I later discovered there was another poor house still standing in nearby Arcadia.

On my way back to Yarmouth from Halifax in the autumn of 1995, I saw that the Digby Almshouse was on fire. It saddened me to think of the events that would have taken place in that building, which was being reduced to ashes before my eyes. I resolved that I would write about that building if I ever had the chance.

Fast-forward 24 years and I am living down the road from the former site of the Marshalltown Almshouse, which had been located outside the Town of Digby. Annapolis Royal had become our home in 1996. With an exhausting career in non-profits, another daughter added to the mix, a marriage, a divorce, a remarriage and the launch of an accidental writing career, I turned my attention back to the Marshalltown Almshouse. By this time, I knew of four former poor houses in Nova Scotia and wanted to learn more. Imagine my astonishment when my research turned up the existence of 32 poor houses in the province in the late 1880s, and at least six even earlier than that.

By the time I started digging into research materials, I knew that the subject of poor houses in Nova Scotia had been touched upon in articles and academic journals and were the focus of one book, published in 1996: *Poverty, Poor Houses and Private Philanthropy*. Written by the Senior Scribes, a group of elderly people who had received a grant to write about these subjects in Nova Scotia, this book was difficult to get my hands on.

In my years of work as an anti-poverty activist, I always considered it important to make sure that the voices of people living in poverty were heard. This is difficult when dealing with historical events. Until recently, history meant the story of elite white males. Few other people were considered worth writing about. Poor people, and especially poor non-white people, rarely had their voices heard. This book offers a faint echo of some of those voices. Although the firsthand experiences of people in Nova Scotia poor houses were not written down, the annual *Reports on Public Charities*, written in the late 19th century, and the *Report on Humanities*, written in the first half of the 20th century, allow us to see inside the houses and some of the experiences of their residents.

The first chapter of this book examines the emergence of poor houses in Nova Scotia and looks at how attitudes toward poor people changed from a sense of Christian charity to blaming poor people for attempting to survive the government and church policies that made them into paupers in the first place. It also looks at how people in Nova Scotia dealt with poverty prior to the arrival of Edward Cornwallis and the British, and the establishment of the first poor house in Halifax. How did the Acadians and Mi'kmaq experience and survive poverty?

The second chapter examines the story of the death of Charlotte Hill and the repercussions of the resulting Poor of Digby enquiry of 1885 on the lives of the poor in Nova Scotia.

Chapter 3 takes a closer look at each of the 32 poor houses in the province.

Chapter 4 examines the treatment of African-Canadians and Mi'kmaq in the poor relief system in Nova Scotia. They received even worse treatment than white poor people because of systemic racism. How did they survive?

Chapter 5 examines the issue of the disabled and the elderly in poor houses. As inmates of poor houses were expected to work for their relief from poverty, what happened to those who could not physically work or were too mentally ill to work for their relief?

Chapter 6 is a look at death in a poor house. What happens when an inmate of a poor house dies? What if there is no family available to claim the body of the pauper? Where were they buried?

Chapter 7 attempts to hear the voices of the poor in the poor houses. Although there are no known records left by a poor house resident, the whispers of their voices is sought from official records, newspapers and interviews.

When you are reading this book, please take off your 21st-century lenses. Many people had a difficult life in the 18th, 19th and early 20th centuries. Many people lived in poverty and did without basic essentials while not living in a poor house. To compare our living standards today to the living standards during those centuries does not make sense. Yes, people in poverty today still have it very difficult; but this book is looking particularly at those who lived in poverty prior to and during the establishment of poor houses.

That is why, in Chapter 8, "Things are So Much Better Now," we put our 21st-century lenses back on. Although standards of living may have improved for people in general in Nova Scotia, we examine how people living in poverty today are still being affected by the attitudes, beliefs and some policies that originated in 16th-century England. These continue to make life for poor people in Nova Scotia "a wholesome horror" even in the 21st century.

Poverty in Early Nova Scotia

A book produced by author Thomas Firman, of England, 1632-1697; Printed by J. Grover, London England and sold by Francis Smith 1681. Image courtesy of Text Creation Partnership, Ann Arbour MI and Oxford (UK) 2008-2009.

Edward Cornwallis looked out over the shimmering water to the forested green hills all around him. He was standing on board the sloop of war the *Sphinx* at the beginning of summer – June 21, 1749. Cornwallis was contemplating the challenges of the task ahead. He had been sent by the British government to establish a town in the harbour the Mi'kmaq called Chebucto, meaning Big Harbour. Even though many British people had come to Nova Scotia before him, Cornwallis was to establish a new town to replace the capital, Annapolis Royal, and to firm up the British presence. This new town, ordered to be settled on the Atlantic side, was to protect the British government's interests and the trade routes of neighbouring New England. Cornwallis was to be the new governor of Nova Scotia in this new town of Halifax.

The *Sphinx* was the first ship to arrive, but the new colonists were only a few days behind. Cornwallis was not just bringing settlers with him to establish the new capital; he was bringing the power of the British Crown and a belief system that would negatively affect many Nova Scotians up until the present day. This belief system was called the Elizabethan Poor Laws.

The Elizabethan Poor Laws, also called An Act for the Relief of the Poor, were enacted as a series of laws between 1552 and 1601.[1] These laws attempted to deal with the fallout of policies from Henry VIII, Elizabeth's father.

When the English king, Henry VIII, fell in love with Anne Boleyn in 1526, he was already married to Catherine of Aragon. Anne, not wanting to be just his mistress with the risk of being put aside after he grew tired of her, insisted that she would only have sexual relations with Henry if she were his wife and queen. Henry took her at her word and changed the course of English history for Anne. One of the things that Henry did to wed Anne was to cut himself off from the Catholic Church of Rome, as traditional Church doctrine did not permit divorce. Henry made himself head of the new Church of England and made it the official religion of his kingdom. This permitted him to divorce Catherine. The marriage to Anne may not have lasted long (three years), but Henry's changes affected millions of people for centuries to come.[2]

As part of establishing himself as head of the Church, by means of the Protestant Reformation Act, Henry ordered the complete destruction of the Catholic monasteries, which he claimed were places of sin.[3] The fact that all the gold, silver and precious stones ended up in his treasury at a time when Henry was almost broke from the costs of his divorce from Catherine of Aragon was a fact not missed by his enemies.

One of the repercussions of the dismantling of the monasteries, however, was to have a disastrous impact on the working people of England. Many townships, hamlets and villages and their citizens relied upon the monasteries for employment, to buy their produce and products, to provide medical assistance and as shelters for travellers. For poor people, the monasteries were a place of refuge; in a monastery, the destitute could receive shelter, food, medicine, and rest.[4] The monasteries had closely adhered to the Bible – Matthew 25 (The Sheep and the Goats), which instructs Christians to feed the hungry, give drink to the thirsty, welcome the stranger, clothe the naked and visit the sick and the prisoner.

The abrupt change in religion and the closure of the monasteries meant that communities were no longer caring for their poor as they no longer had the nuns, the monks and the means to do this. When Henry ordered the dismantling of these religious institutions, he threw many people into unemployment. He put their businesses and farms into ruin and he took away the only refuge for poor and sick people. He turned many of his citizens into paupers and beggars.

As a result, poor people moved from their rural homes into more urban areas looking for work to support themselves and their families. When they could not find work, they turned to prostitution, stealing and begging.[5] These were their only means of survival in Henry VIII's time.

Henry VIII did not take this spread of poverty in his kingdom very well. The king and his advisors decided to deal with the poor through punishing their "idleness." This policy became known as the Tudor Poor Laws, or the Vagabonds and Beggars Act of 1494.[6] If a citizen was found begging, they would be put in the stocks. If a poor citizen was found outside their hamlet, village, or town without work, they would be whipped through the streets and returned to their community. If the citizen returned to the town and was caught again, they would lose an ear. If they returned a third time, they would be executed.[7]

By the time Queen Elizabeth I, daughter of Henry VIII, came to the throne in 1558, the poor people of England had become more numerous and an even greater problem. There was a threat of civil war against the monarchy that had put them in poverty. A few years of failed harvests, along with a tremendous increase in population meant that a great number of the citizenry were in dire straits. Elizabeth and her advisors decided to handle the "poverty problem" with the new Act for the Relief of the Poor, which became known as the Elizabethan Poor Laws.[8]

Under this new legislation, parishes, a territorial area of the local church, became the administrative unit responsible for putting the Poor Law into effect. Two overseers of the poor were appointed to each parish to take care of the parish's poor people. The idea was to move away from punishing the poor and move more toward "correcting" the poor.[9] To achieve this, Elizabeth's Poor Laws had four main aspects:

1. Those poor who could not work due to advanced age or illnesses such as blindness or lameness were to be housed in an "almshouse," also known as a "poor house." (see definition p. 56)
2. The able-bodied poor, those who could work but could not find work, would be sent to work in a house of industry, also known as a workhouse, to earn their keep of food, clothing, and shelter.
3. The "idle poor," those who were unwilling to work for their keep, would be sent to a house of correction, or prison. These included "vagrants" and "beggars."
4. Poor children would become apprentices and learn a trade.[10]

Under the Elizabethan Poor Laws, relief could come in two forms: indoor relief and outdoor relief. Indoor relief was life inside a poor house; outdoor relief was life outside the poor house and could include food, clothing, coal or wood, and sometimes money. Because of these new laws, almshouses, houses of industry and houses of correction were built to house the poor of England. Almshouses were supported by local churches of the same denomination; Houses of Industry were also called Work Houses and residents of these buildings were expected to work for the House for their keep. Houses of Correction were not just for criminals but also for those people who did not follow the unwritten societal norms of their communities. Poor Houses and poor farms were for those who no longer had a place to live, the ability to live within their own homes or family that were willing to take care of them if they were elderly or ill.

The type of relief a person received depended upon the type of poverty they were in; elderly people on their own usually received indoor relief – the poor house. Families that were experiencing temporary unemployment would often receive outdoor relief. Families were also made responsible for their members who were poor. Children must take care of their parents as parents once took care of their children.[11]

To fund the Poor Laws, monies were raised in the form of tax levies. The overseers of the poor would collect these taxes from people residing in the parish and, in turn, these taxes paid not only for the overseers, but also for the building, maintenance and staffing of the poor house and the outdoor relief needed by other families within the parish.[12]

Whenever a person became poor or was born into poverty, their parish became responsible for keeping them from starvation. If a poor person attempted to move to another town or parish and was still poor, the new parish was not permitted to help them. Instead, the parish was required to send the poor person back to their own parish and request poor help there.[13] Some parishes were wealthy enough to help their destitute, but often the parish itself was poor as a result of famine, floods, or drought and was not able to help the poor person and their family.

Along with this more "gentle approach" to people in poverty came the shift away from the Christian Bible – Matthew Chapter 25 to Thessalonians 3:9 – 10: "If anyone is not willing to work, neither shall he eat," which put the responsibility for living in poverty squarely onto the shoulders of the poor person. This shift to the Protestant work ethic focused on the concept that through hard work, thrift and adherence to the Protestant faith, the faithful could have a life that would result in wealth, happiness and God's favour.

The writing group Senior Scribes examine this same issue in *Poverty, Poor Houses and Private Philanthropy:*

> Poverty and its attendant evils were viewed as being associated with flaws in character and morals: the inevitable consequence of sin and disobedience against the will of God. Work and industry were considered virtues, *at least for the poor*; unwillingness to work, indeed, very often, inability to work, was labelled laziness and considered a cardinal sin. (emphasis mine)[14]

Although these new Poor Laws were not as harsh as the ones under Henry VIII and provided the destitute with some form of shelter and relief, they also promoted the idea that the poor were in conditions of poverty through some fault of their own. This is an idea we still hold today. This was an important shift in ideas; the general public came to view the poor as responsible for their own poverty through their bad decision-making, idleness, alcohol addiction, or "repudiating the Protestant Work Ethic."[15]

The idea that floods, drought, community and family tragedies, harsh government and church policies and the like may push them into poverty was not open to exploration by those in power. Instead, the "deviance" of the idle, the addicts and the unwed mothers attracted the attention of the criminal and civil law. The "deserving poor", as a result, came to comprise a limited group of people, consisting mainly of widows and temporarily unemployed workers with families.[16] The system was ripe for abuse of the poor, and for fraud and misuse of funds by those trusted with the monies raised through the poor taxes.

Over the centuries, almshouses, poor houses, and houses of industry were built in England and filled with the misery of humans who had the misfortune of being poor. Once a person entered the poor house, they gave up their freedom to come and go as they pleased, the opportunities to make their own decisions and, often, their families. Resident of poor houses became known as "inmates," and they were expected to earn their own keep within the institution. Able-bodied men, women and children were put to work for up to twelve hours a day.[17] Men often had to break stone for roads and buildings, while women either worked in the kitchen, the infirmary section of the poor house, or with the children picking oakum out of rope.[18] The Senior Scribes write about a work house in Shelburne, Nova Scotia:

In Shelburne in 1786 the Master of the Workhouse would have inmates pick oakum, clean streets and build wharves. He requested authority to put shackles and fetters on inmates and punish them by whipping.

A great stigma was attached to anyone residing in the poor house or even threatened with being put in the poor house. In the first years of the poor houses, they were used as a deterrent against the "idleness" of the poor. The buildings were designed to be intimidating, imposing, and institutional: "The applicant was 'offered the house', and it was assumed that no able-bodied person would accept this form of assistance because of the horrible conditions in the workhouse. Later, when the workhouse was finally abolished, the poor house was used in much the same way."[19]

The poor house and the change in attitudes towards poor people, which not only blamed them for their poverty but also aligned them with criminals, resulted in the control and regulation of those in poverty to prevent them from rising up in arms against those in wealth. Judith Fingard writes: "The spectre of hungry mobs of workers conjured up in the mind of the authorities frightening thoughts of uncontrollable outrage and seething insubordination."[20] The 17th-century English proverb "A hungry man is an angry man" would have also contributed to this fear. Charles Dickens wrote his classic novel *Oliver Twist* about a boy who was born in a work house, and Benjamin Disraeli wrote *Sybil*, also known as *The Two Nations*, with a similar theme.[21]

Governor Cornwallis checked over the length and breadth of Chebucto Harbour and decided to settle the new town of Halifax at a cove at the bottom of a large hill. Within weeks, log cabins and government buildings were erected. Cornwallis, being a man of his time and upbringing, organized the government with like-minded men and began to pass bills to institute laws. Within a few short years, the first poor house would be built in Halifax, based on the model of the Elizabethan almshouses in London. The peers of Cornwallis passed a bill in 1759 called *An Act for Erecting a House of Correction or Work House within the Town of Halifax*.[22] In this act, they decreed that persons coming into the poor house and house of corrections (the two were in one building) would be subjected to "moderate whipping" for being "stubborn or idle and neglecting to perform such reasonable tasks as shall be assigned them, and to abridge them of their food, as the case may require, until they be reduced to better behaviour."[23]

Thus, the Elizabethan Poor Laws came to Nova Scotia, but because many communities could not afford to erect a poor house, the practice of auctioning off the poor began. Historian A.W.H. Eaton writes:

> For many years it was customary for certain ratepayers to "bid off" one or more poor men, women or children for stipulated sums to be paid weekly by the town ... the ratepayers made the poor whom they bidded (sic) off, useful in their homes; for such service and for the sum they received, giving the unfortunates board, lodging and clothes. Many persons also, who became town charges were "farmed out" to men who made their living wholly or in part by boarding them.[24]

This was the beginning of a huge paradigm shift in attitudes towards poor people in Nova Scotia. The Elizabethan Poor Laws were formally in place in Nova Scotia until 1958, when they were officially repealed by the provincial government. The attitudes and beliefs which were the result of the Elizabethan Poor Laws, however, would persist and would have an impact on Nova Scotia's citizens for centuries to come.

Before the arrival of Cornwallis and his British settlers in the new town of Halifax, poverty was dealt with in a completely different manner than it was under the Elizabethan Poor Laws. Prior to the adoption of these laws, there was no tradition of government responsibility for the poor. The Mi'kmaq, who had not developed or participated in a fiat monetary system, did not know poverty. They knew of bad fishing and hunting seasons and times of famine, but poverty, as defined by Europeans, was unknown to them. Mi'kmaq historian Daniel Paul writes: "Notions of personal property and obligations to pay debts owed to another were alien to Amerindian thinking and it took the People a long time to accustom themselves to them."[25]

Of the Acadians, who had been living mainly along the Bay of Fundy and who associated with the Mi'kmaq a great deal, Jean Daigle writes:

> Limited immigration to Acadia meant that, after three or four generations, all inhabitants of the various settlements were related to one another (uncle, cousin, distant cousin) etc. As is always the case in this type of rural society, the emotional and blood ties created by kinship formed a basis for the establishment of a system of mutual aid, solidarity

and independence, in which the wealthier distributed their surplus to those whom war or natural disaster had touched. This homogeneity created what is commonly called the Acadian extended family, a traditional society that was able to resist the great social upheavals of the period, thanks to its natural resources.[26]

The Mi'kmaq did not lock up their food or hoard it as the Europeans did. They shared their resources amongst their group of people and often helped people outside of their group, such as the Acadians and other Europeans. Membertou demonstrated this sharing culture of the Mi'kmaq when the French explorers first arrived to settle Port Royal in 1604. The Mi'kmaq welcomed them and helped them make it through the winter with gifts of food, such as fresh meat. Daniel Paul describes how European cultures were so different from this:

> European civilizations of the day ... used a totalitarian approach. This was a direct result of the fact that they were governed by a titled elite who considered themselves to have a divine right to rule ... Because of this elitism, average citizens within these domains were routinely denied basic human rights and freedoms.[27]

The Acadians and Mi'kmaq often intermarried and had children. In 1755, just a few short years after the arrival of Cornwallis and the British, Governor Lawrence ordered the Grand Dérangement of all Acadians. The Mi'kmaq managed to warn some of the Acadian families of the imminent expulsion and helped them to hide in the woods, keeping them safe and helping them with the provision of food throughout the succeeding winters until the British called off the expulsion in 1764.

This is not to suggest that Acadians did not suffer from poverty prior to the Expulsion, but as Roman Catholics they looked to the church for assistance as well as to their neighbours. At the end of the expulsion, some Acadians made their way back to Nova Scotia. They found that their farms were either burned and left fallow or taken over by the British and New Englanders.[28] No compensation was ever paid to them for these losses. As a result, many of the Acadians ended up in the same poverty as some of the new settlers to Nova Scotia.

Chapter 2

---·—·---

The Death of Charlotte Hill and the Early Poor Houses

Charlotte Hill was 29 years old, short with stooped shoulders, a thin face and several missing front teeth. By all accounts her appearance had been hardened by a life of poverty. At six months pregnant, she climbed into the ox-drawn cart that early morning of August 31, 1880, without the help of Joe Tibo. Tibo believed in doing things yourself and so he did not lend Charlotte a hand despite her growing girth.

The sun had not yet risen and the air was chilly. Joe tended to be a silent man and this morning was no different. As the oxen pulled the cart out of North Range in the County of Digby, through the village of Bear River and into the back woods of Annapolis County, Charlotte thought about the child she would have by Christmas. She knew that she would be allowed to keep the baby for a year — time enough to nurse and love the infant and then to give the baby to the overseers of the poor. Her unborn child, like the previous four she had birthed, would be raised by another family as their servant or labourer ... just as she had been.

Charlotte was one of eight children born to Mary Purdy, who was unmarried. As there was no support for unwed mothers, Mary also had to give her children up to the overseers. Charlotte was raised in the houses of whomever offered to feed and clothe her for the least amount of money. Although they didn't do "poor auctions" in Digby County any longer, as they had in the days of her mother, the overseers did ask "respectable" residents to bid on the poor people of the area, and the lowest bid usually meant that family got the poor person to work for them for a year. But if the poor person was old, "insane", disabled, or very pregnant, they were considered less valuable because they could not work.

Tibo told her that he was taking her to another family, in Middlefield, Queens County, which would keep her even though she was pregnant. Charlotte did not argue with Tibo about this; she knew what he was capable of. He may have been well respected by his business peers in the Town of Digby, but she had seen Tibo horsewhip other poor people in his charge. But it upset her greatly that she was being moved far away from her best friend, Anita Scott. She and Anita had been through difficult times together and helped each other out as much as they could. Anita had saved Charlotte from throwing herself off the barn roof in an attempt to kill herself. Life for them was difficult and miserable. They were the paupers — the undesirables of Digby County.

As the ox cart passed by the hamlet of Victory on the Greenfield road, Tibo finally began to talk about stopping and making a fire for something to eat. Isaiah Munro was just waking up from his lunchtime nap on a soft patch of moss. He was picking up his scythe to do some more haying in his field when he saw a plume of dark smoke not far away. Muttering to himself about the danger of a fire that size, Isaiah put down the scythe and went to investigate. After all, he didn't want it spreading to his field and burning all his crops. As Isaiah hurried toward the fire, he passed a man in an ox cart hurrying in the opposite direction from the fire. Isaiah recognized him as Joe Tibo, a man he had spoken with often while doing business in Bear River.

Isaiah finally located the fire on the edge of a bog. He immediately saw that there were brush and rocks on the fire ... and a human foot sticking out from the blaze. Feeling sick with the smell of burning flesh, Munro put the fire out as best he could and ran to contact the authorities.

After the police and the coroner from nearby Annapolis Royal arrived, Dr. Bingay removed the rest of the stones and brush to discover a woman's body underneath. Although her legs had been completely burnt, her torso and face were intact and she was still recognizable as Charlotte Hill. Her pregnancy was also apparent. Upon examination of the remains of Charlotte's body, Dr. Bingay believed that she had been alive when she was consumed by the fire.

The police came for Joe Tibo as he knew they would. He sat with his wife in the kitchen of their farm house and waited for them. He knew that he had been seen by Munro as he got out of the area as fast as he could that day in August. It took the authorities three days to come for him.

Tibo protested that he was an innocent man. He claimed that he had not pushed Charlotte into the fire but rather that she had thrown herself upon the flames in a fit of depression. He argued that he was a respected man in the community. When the authorities found Tibo's ox cart hidden on his property under fir boughs, it confirmed his guilt in their minds. Why would a person hide their cart if they were not guilty? As word of Tibo's arrest spread, an angry mob gathered. They were upset that a man who was supposed to be respectable and taking care of the poor had done such a barbarous act to one of his wards.

The trial of 45-year-old businessman Joseph Tibo began on December 1, 1880, in a packed courtroom in Annapolis Royal. There were newspaper reporters from all over the province, as well as from New Brunswick. Tibo's lawyer, Robert Motton, argued that Charlotte had thrown herself into the fire as she was in despair about being pregnant and not married for the fifth time and being moved away from her best friend. Her friend Anita took the stand and testified about how she had saved Charlotte from jumping off the barn roof. She testified that her best friend was very upset at leaving Joe Tibo's North Range farm, where they lived in a "rough but comfortable manner" and going to a new place where she had no friends.

Motton also argued that his client was a smart man and would not have been seen out and about with Charlotte if he had intended to murder her. The prosecutor, John Thompson, who went on to become the premier of Nova Scotia, a justice in the provincial Supreme Court, the federal justice minister and finally the prime minister, sternly replied to this allegation: "Men are never wise when they resort to crime. Innocence is the only wisdom."

The prosecution argued that Joe Tibo was no doubt the father of Charlotte's baby and did not want it to be born at his farm, where the similarities between himself, his other children and this child would become apparent. They alleged that Tibo had every intention of making sure the baby would not be born at all and that Charlotte would not be able to talk about the father of this baby either. The prosecution accused Joe Tibo of throwing Charlotte into the fire.

On the last day of the trial, December 6, the jury were sent to a private room to discuss the evidence and determine the guilt or innocence of Joseph Tibo. A short two hours later, the jury returned with a verdict of guilty. Tibo's date of execution by hanging was set for February 8, 1881.

As hangings were no longer public, a tall fence was erected around the gallows for Tibo's hanging. However, a large crowd of spectators had gathered to watch and, angry that they would be denied this spectacle, they knocked down the fence. The judge, reporters, and lawyers all watched from the courthouse windows. It took 14 minutes for the condemned man to die.

Did Joe Tibo throw Charlotte Hill into the fire or did Charlotte commit suicide, as Tibo's lawyer suggested? Was an innocent man hanged or was a poor house inmate murdered? We will ever know the truth. However, the newspaper publicity surrounding this case brought to light how the County of Digby treated its poor citizens. Rumours, whispers and stories became widespread to the point where reports began appearing in newspapers in Halifax and even Ottawa, with "several charges of maladministration of the poor laws and of certain horrible barbarities alleged to have been perpetrated on the poor of the County of Digby."[29]

Public outcry led to the establishment in 1885 of an official enquiry by the Legislature of Nova Scotia. Entitled *The Poor of Digby*, the enquiry's mandate included investigating what had happened to Charlotte Hill and how Joseph Tibo had treated the poor people in his care. A final report was written for the Legislature by Commissioner Francis H. Bell in 1886.[30]

The enquiry investigated the following allegations:

1. That the "poor are once a year put up at public auction and sold as slaves to the lowest bidder."
2. That "our indigent poor" are treated with cruelty.
3. That the practice of "farming or selling our poor to the lowest bidder" prevails.
4. That the poor in the County of Digby are considered "beneath notice and are treated as worse than worn out or useless animals."
5. That we have "no organized system of relief or protection of any kind for our poor."
6. That the result is "semi-nakedness, semi-starvation, misery, cruelty, outrage, and murder."
7. That as soon as the "poor creatures are knocked down to the lowest bidder they become their property, without appeal, and are led off to labor, in most instances to a premature death."
8. That our poor are "subjected to every species of cruelty, from the ordinary kick and blow to the murderous bludgeon."
9. That "our poor are led away to die in the backwoods and out of the way places, and that if these places could tell their own tales we would have

an endless list of cruelties and brutal crimes to ponder over."

10. That a fellow citizen would, if he had dared, have knocked one pauper on the head to get rid of him.
11. That 25 paupers were sold to one man for $125 (afterwards put at $550) and that this man makes considerable profit out of the labor of his "slave gang."
12. That the overseers of the poor permitted an old woman to be "gradually deformed by want, cold and suffering."
13. That "an old woman lay in the barn with the cattle, a mass of filth, disease and pain."
14. That they permitted an old Waterloo veteran to "approach his grave in cold and need."
15. That the overseers of the poor pay no attention to the poor from the day they "sell" them to the "lowest bidder" till the day of their death.
16. That our overseers of the poor carry on "an immoral traffic which hardly bears description."
17. That the overseers of the poor "do not part with the poor until they find the lowest bidder."[31]

E.R. Oakes, John McNeill and Henry Robichau had gathered these allegations from the newspaper reports and requested the Lieutenant Governor in Council to appoint an enquiry to investigate these charges. The purpose of the enquiry was too look at these allegations and, if found guilty, to punish the perpetrators of the abuse. Beginning on Wednesday, September 9 and ending the afternoon of Tuesday, September 15, the enquiry examined more than 50 witnesses.[32]

F.H. Bell makes clear that in his opinion the case of Charlotte Hill should not be included in the enquiry as it had been investigated thoroughly at the time of the trial of Joe Tibo. However, because the death of Charlotte Hill was the launching point into the allegations of mistreatment of the poor in Digby County, Bell covered the major aspects of Hill's time within the poor relief system and then moved on to investigate complaints made by and about other poor relief recipients.

Bell investigated the allegations by talking with the poor masters, neighbours, other poor relief recipients in the area and the recipients who were named. However, Bell interviewed the poor relief recipients in front of their keepers!

The recipients dared not blame their keepers for abuse in fear of what would happen once Bell left the home. Fingers of blame were most often pointed back to the poor themselves for neglecting to ask for help when they needed it.

In examining the sale of the poor of Digby County, Bell determined that the overseers of the poor chose the places where the poor were to be lodged each year and made a bargain for that purpose:

> There is nothing at all in the nature of a sale at auction. I may say here that the custom of selling the poor at auction undoubtedly did prevail in the county at one time but has now for some years past been abandoned in all the poor districts. The date of the abandonment differs in the different sections. Some dropped the practice as much as thirty years ago. The latest instance appears to have been in the Plympton district some ten years ago.[33]

Member of Provincial Parliament Jonathan S. McNeil resorts to double speak when he says that rather than a "sale" of the poor, it is more a "contract for maintenance."[34] He also notes that the poor masters were free to subcontract out their poor to a third party and that the overseers of the poor for each district had no control over who the third party might be.[35]

However, author Malcolm Cecil Foster wrote in his memoirs of the auctions that took place around the same time in the farming community of Clarence (which the writer attempts to disguise by referring to it as Clifton, which is approximately 50 kilometers down the road), in neighbouring Annapolis County:

> Not all of the poor of those days were on the road as tramps. Every Ward had a rather generous supply of the stationary down-and-out; and since there was no poor house, the Ward was compelled to make its own arrangements for their care, that is, with the help of County funds. So once a year (it was usually in the summertime) the poor were auctioned off to the lowest bidder in order that the taxpayers would have as little to pay as possible. I understand the same custom prevailed for some time up in New England ... As a boy those auctions were downright revolting to me, and to many others of that time; and from the more humane viewpoint of today they appear even worse. They were, of course, the *only* means provided for the care of our poor and our harmless insane, and I suppose

we did the best we could in the absence of any better method. We weren't unconcerned about their welfare. Yet as these "sales" were conducted in Clifton there was room for considerable improvement, particularly on the part of the auctioneer. Were they much above the level of a sale of livestock? I'll let you be the judge. A two-year-old steer doesn't understand the *complimentary* things that are said about him. The poor human derelicts who were on the block understood the *uncomplimentary* remarks which couldn't fail to reach their ears.[36]

After concluding that no such poor auctions were ongoing in Digby County, Bell does question some of the behind-the-scenes arrangements being made between local shopkeepers and poor masters that were not in the best interests of the poor:

The overseers, indemnifiers (poor masters) and councillors (municipal) play into one another's hands so as to make the appropriations for relief and the appointments as indemnifiers to suit themselves, and that the result of such must be log rolling and improper expenditure.[37]

On the question of building a poor house, Bell tells readers to decide for themselves whether that would be more cost effective. But then he strongly urges them to examine the "greater cheapness and saving to be effected (sic) by the establishment of a poor house is drawn from the county of Annapolis."[38] The brand new poor house outside of Bridgetown, Annapolis County, had been established in 1881, only four years prior to this enquiry.

Senior Scribes write that there were five poor houses in the province prior to 1879: one in Halifax, two in Kings County, one in Antigonish County and one in Yarmouth County. They write as well that it appeared that there were poor houses in both Shelburne and Queens Counties prior to 1879, the year of the passage of the County Incorporation Act, after which counties became responsible for their own poor and "insane."[39] As research evolved, more former poor houses came to light. Senior Scribes also refer to a poor house in North Range in Digby County but admit they cannot find much information about it.[40]

Historian Dr. Allan Marble, in his book *Physicians, Pestilence, and the Poor*, writes that there were five poor houses in the rural parts of the province prior to 1880. He locates them in Shelburne, Chebogue in Yarmouth County,

Clementsport in Annapolis County, and the towns of Antigonish and Pictou.[41]

Adding the numbers in these accounts together, it appears there were nine poor houses in the province prior to 1879. Further research uncovered another poor house, in Beaconsfield, outside of the town of Bridgetown, which boarded poor people and orphans in the 1840s.[42] It is not known how long it was in operation.

Shelburne County, in southeast Nova Scotia, established its poor house and work house combination in 1783. It was year the American Revolutionary War ended, and Shelburne was crowded with Loyalist refugees, both white and black. The Loyalists quickly established a poor house and house of corrections, where both poor and criminal were housed side by side. The weekly rations, as described by the poor keeper, consisted of "three pounds of Indian Meal, three pounds of Salt fish, six quarts of Potatoes."[43] This poor house was located on Harriot Street and operated until at least 1806. In that year, the overseers of the poor proposed that the poor be gathered together and put in some place by themselves as the existing poor house was not in a condition to receive them.[44]

Antigonish opened a poor house in the Old Court House, on the corner of Pleasant and Acadia Street, which began receiving poor inmates on May 1, 1860. *The Third Annual Report of the Poor House*, written by Poor House Keeper Neil McKenna and printed in the *Casket* newspaper on April 9, 1863, illustrates how the poor were treated in that poor house and general area. McKenna notes that prior to the opening of the poor house, the county was supporting sixteen paupers and that three years later it was supporting, on average, eight paupers. In section 4 of his report, McKenna concludes:

> The operation of the Poor house system for the past three years has therefore convinced us that the only proper objects for public sympa-thy and aid, are those who consent to become inmates of the Asylum for the time being; for it is now self-evident that we cannot protect ourselves against the claims of sham paupers by any other method.[45]

McKenna's report shows that Antigonish County no longer offered outdoor assistance of food, wood or coal and clothing to the residents of that county; if a person needed help, they had to live in the poor house. The fear of incarcera-tion in the poor house kept many "sham paupers" from taking money they "did not deserve" from the good taxpayers of Antigonish County.

Yarmouth established a poor house and farm at Chebogue in 1857. J.M. Lawson, author of *Yarmouth Past and Present*, writes:

> A Public Meeting was held on the 24th June, 1857, to consider the propriety of taxing the town for land and building a Home for the Poor. A resolution was passed, and the farm of John Richards, Chebogue, was selected by a committee appointed for the purpose and purchased for £500. The building was opened in August of that year, but was soon found to be inadequate for the purpose. It was sold at auction and was purchased by John K. Ryerson.[46]

Another poor house was opened in Arcadia, Yarmouth County, but not until 1870, nine years before the 1879 County Incorporation Act.

May 1850 saw the residents of Clementsport, under the guidance of Rev. W. Godfrey, petition the province for "the building of a Poor House and the suppression of vagrancy."[47] Indeed, a poor house was built on what is now called the Shaw Road and was intended solely for the benefit of the township of Clements. Overseen by Poor Master Anthony Potter, the facility recorded housing as many as 80 inmates there at the same time.[48]

Allan Marble writes that in 1861 the Town of Pictou established a poor house, which was described by a writer in the *Eastern Chronicle* on May 2 of that year, as "commodious and comfortable."[49] The Senior Scribes, however, provide a different date, reporting that in 1863 the Poor Committee of the Town of Pictou recommended that the town establish its own poor house.[50]

There is conflicting information about the Queens County poor house as well. In 1797, Liverpool diarist Simeon Perkins notes that the Town approved £125 for a poor house. However, in 1819, the Proprietors Meeting voted "that the Poor of this town be let at Auction at a day appointed by the Overseers of the Poor." In the middle

The A.F. Church map, 1871, shows the location of the poor house in Clementsport.

of the century, Jedidiah Gorham offered to give £100 "toward the erection of a Poor house," but the offer was declined.[51]

Perhaps the facilities in Queens County, Pictou, North Range and Beaconsfield were all private poor houses, with the poor masters having purchased the paupers during one of the auctions and brought them to their homes to work. Allan Marble writes:

Outside of Halifax, townships of 50 or more families were, in November 1763, empowered by the Legislature to maintain their poor through assessment of poor rates ... Needless to say the ratepayer who took a pauper not only boarded him or her but, in most cases, required the pauper to carry out an inordinate amount of work.[52]

Several communities applied to the province for assistance in building a poor house but were either unsuccessful in their bid or received the funding but did not build the poor house. Annapolis Royal petitioned for funding four times.

In 1815, a plan was drawn up by John Edson for a "Workhouse and Poor House on Hogg Island, near the Town of Annapolis to be built of brick and lime," and £6000 was allocated for this purpose. The Grand Jury of the County appointed Phineas Lovett, Thomas Ritchie and Captain Isaac Woodbury as commissioners to contract for materials. In 1821, the Grand Jury made notice that "the materials for building a County Poor House on Hogg Island to be sold for the benefit of the County and each Township shall receive an equal portion of the same."[53] The men appointed to sell these materials, Laurence Sneden, Thomas Ritchie and Major Gesner were also assigned to "examine the accounts of the former Commissioners."[54] It is interesting that Thomas Ritchie was appointed to oversee his previous work as a commissioner. Perhaps it was a different Thomas Ritchie as the Ritchie family of the area was prolific and, like other families, used the same names repeatedly. Annapolis County continued to petition unsuccessfully for money for a poor house – in 1844, 1850 and 1852.

Clements Township petitioned the provincial government unsuccessfully in 1807, 1817 and 1858. Finally, in 1867, permission was granted and their poor house was built, as mentioned previously, on what is now called Shaw Road.

Allan Marble refers to one of the earliest private poor houses as belonging to Benjamin K. Dodge, of Granville Township:

He took charge of fifteen paupers by a contract with the Overseers of the Poor in that Township on 3 April 1837. Dodge was required to provide paupers with "sufficient meal and drink, washing, lodging, and wearing apparel, and all other necessities in sickness and in health, for one year for a sum of £112 plus Court costs."[55]

There were other private poor houses in the province during the 1840s and 1850s, including two run by William G. Lavers and William Mixner of Windsor. Alexander Buchanan successfully bid on 19 paupers in Horton for £125 and Benjamin Cole bid on 17 paupers in Liverpool Township in 1851 for £179. James Delap contracted to care for 25 paupers in Granville Township for £192. Many of these paupers were subcontracted out to board and work at other farms or residences, with the successful bidders realizing a profit on their human purchases.[57]

According to Allan Marble, another ten proposals to erect poor houses were made but did not reach fruition because the funds needed for such endeavours could not be raised from the community poor rates.[58] In addition to raising the necessary funds to build a poor house, the petitioners were up against a prevalent belief that poor houses were not good for the paupers in them. It was believed that "a pauper would suffer more abuse in a Poor House from the keeper and from other paupers than if resident in a private home."[59]

The County of Digby did eventually erect its own poor house after the enquiry of 1885, outside of the town of Digby in the community of Marshalltown. In his 1886 report, Commissioner Francis H. Bell dismissed the 17 allegations of "cruel and barbarous" treatment as unfounded.[60] Treatment of the poor in Nova Scotia began to change around this time. Indeed, the Poor of Digby Enquiry, along with several other events regarding poor people in Nova Scotia, shifted some attitudes and led to a great many changes for the poor people in this province. But despite all these good intentions toward the poor, not all of the changes were good.

Chapter 3

Poor Houses in Nova Scotia

"Prison, with a milder name,
Which few inhabit without dread or shame."
~George Crabbe, in his poem "The Borough," published in 1810

There were poor houses in every county in Nova Scotia except Guysborough. Some counties, such as Kings and Yarmouth, had more than one. In the case of Digby County, the poor farm and almshouse in Marshalltown housed mainly English-speaking inmates, while the poor house in Meteghan, in the District of Clare, housed mainly Acadian/French-speaking inmates.

A poor person did not just walk into a poor house and expect to be taken in. Usually, they had to give a letter of reference to the poor keeper written by someone of status or importance in the area. Once the poor people were accepted into the poor house, if they were a couple or a family, they could expect to be immediately split up. Wives were separated from husbands and children were separated from parents. There would be no leaving the poor house grounds without permission from the poor keeper.

Dr. G.L. Sinclair and Dr. A.C. Page were both medical doctors in Nova Scotia who were tasked with the job of making inspections of all poor houses in Nova Scotia. This meant travelling all over Nova Scotia, to every county that had a poor house and doing an inspection, not only of the state of the buildings, but also of the inmates and their conditions. The Inspectors were to see that the provincial standards and policies, such as the installation of fire escapes, were implemented despite the fact that the poor houses were funded by the municipalities. They were to make recommendations of any improvements and see that the Poor Masters and Overseers of the poor were doing their jobs. The Inspectors provided an annual written report to the Legislature which has given us a wealth of historical information to draw upon.

The keepers and staff of the poor houses often did their best with the resources available to them, considering the cultural and community beliefs about poor people in those days and with the availability of the inmates to work in poor houses and on poor farms. Some poor keepers did their best to maintain and house the poor in a dignified and respectful manner, while others disregarded such niceties and were abusive towards their charges.

Annapolis County Poor Farm, Bridgetown

Annapolis County Poor Farm, outside of Bridgetown. From the Richard McCully Aerial Photograph Collection, 1931, 2012-101/001 no. 38. Used with permission of the Public Archives of Nova Scotia.

The Annapolis County Poor Farm had the dubious distinction of being the only poor facility in the province to segregate African-Nova Scotian paupers from white Nova Scotian paupers. Built in 1885 for the purpose of sheltering and caring for the poor and "harmless insane" of the area, the Annapolis County Poor House was a "poorly ventilated brick building" with "too many narrow dark passageways which, like the rooms, require the services of the plasterer and painter."[61] Annapolis County had been attempting to have a poor house built since 1815; however, it took 80 years before the institution was constructed, 1.6 kilometres outside of Bridgetown.

Dr. Page notes in 1889 that there were 42 inmates in a building that was "75 to 80 feet long and 32 feet wide and four stories high." He also recommends in his report that one of the inmates, "young Bennett," should be moved to Mount Hope Asylum outside of Dartmouth:

He frequently parades the streets with a gun or an ax on his shoulder, a terror to many of the inhabitants.... recently went to the Penitentiary for the criminal assault on one of the inmates – a half-witted girl.[62]

In 1890, Dr. Sinclair reports:

Two of the insane men are profane, dangerous and generally base. One of the insane women recently jumped out of a third storey window and landed without serious injury to her body or benefit to her mind ....
S.B., an epileptic, is very violent and dangerous at times.[63]

In 1897, a "Colored Home" was established to house the African-Nova Scotian paupers who were seeking help from the Annapolis County Poor Farm.[64]

In 1926, Dr. A.C. Jost was the inspector of humane institutions. He put the Annapolis County Poor House and Asylum, as it was then called, into Class 1, which indicates that only the mentally ill were cared for there and that all equipment, sanitary conditions and staff were in place for this mandate.

The Social Assistance Act of 1958 brought about sweeping changes and, although financial assistance to unwed mothers was not included, the new approach to caring for the mentally ill, the poor and children meant that the poor farm was no longer needed. In 1966 the building was torn down and a new building erected; Mountain Lea Lodge and the Meadows were built to provide care for seniors and people who were mentally challenged.[65]

Antigonish Poor Farm and Asylum

The Antigonish Poor Farm and Asylum was one of the few poor houses that were around prior to the County Incorporation Act of 1879. The first poor house in Antigonish had been in existence since 1860 in the old Court House and the second one was located on St. Ninian Street, on the outskirts of the town.[66]

In his 1888 annual report, the inspector of public charities, Dr. A.C. Page, notes that the St. Ninian Street poor house was close to being overcrowded.[67] In 1890 Dr. Page observes that the house was very crowded, with 21 inmates living there: "The long-promised farm with new building will come soon, I hope. The new building must come, or the present one be enlarged, for it is now filled to its utmost capacity."[68]

In his report of 1891, Dr. Page notes that he visited the old poor house on St. Ninian Street on July 7th and expresses his displeasure that an "illegitimate child" had been born there during the year. He admonishes the establishment for not keeping the sexes separate.[69]

In the same report, Dr. Page describes visiting the Antigonish Poor Farm and Asylum for the purpose of looking at the new buildings:

I visited again on December 28th and 29th for the purpose of inspecting the Poor Farm, purchased recently, and the buildings erected thereon. The farm of thirty acres with small house on it is pleasantly located about one and a half miles from the town and cost sixteen hundred dollars. Two new buildings have been erected, one 50x35, the other 40x30.

This house and buildings remained the Antigonish Poor Farm and Asylum until it burned down in 1947. Fortunately, no lives were lost. The institution was never replaced, and the patients were moved to the asylums in Pugwash and Cole Harbour.[70] As an interesting note, Dr. Blois was the deputy minister of public welfare at the time of the fire. Upon hearing of the burning of the institution, he allegedly commented that the fire was a good thing because all the lice, fleas, rats and bedbugs in Antigonish County would have been consumed in it. He believed, apparently, that only those who were poor harboured such vermin.[71]

The Municipal Home Monday afternoon.

TINA COMEAU PHOTO

Old poor farm is no more

by TINA COMEAU
Vanguard Staff Writer

On Monday afternoon a part of Yarmouth County's past became history with the demolition of the old "poor farm" in Arcadia.

The building, also called the poor asylum, was originally built by the municipality in 1870 to house the poor but over the years became a home to those with mental or physical challenges.

Arcadia resident Ruth Pinner, who rents the dwelling house which up until Monday afternoon was located adjacent to the former municipal home, watched the demolition of the building with mixed emotions. While it operated, Pinner had worked at the home for about a year.

"I'm going to miss it so," she said.

The building operated as a working farm until the 1970s, when changes in government policy led to its closure. The residents of the home were moved to other facilities like Harbourside Lodge.

Pinner says it is sad to see the building go because of its history and the memories associated with it, but from a safety perspective she feels the demolition is probably for the best.

"There was always concern that someone was going to start a fire as a prank," she says. The building has been abandoned for years. Pinner says safety issues also weighed heavy on the mind of the building's owner.

The owner of the property had applied for a demolition permit, but at the time of the demolition Monday the permit had not yet been issued, although the fee had been paid. Building inspector Brad Fulton says despite the fact the demolition went ahead without the permit, no municipal bylaws were violated. Fulton says the permit had not yet been "technically" issued but the municipality had no reason to deny the application. He says they had only held off issuing the permit at the request of the heritage committee, which wanted an opportunity to discuss the proposed demolition first.

The Municipal Home early Monday morning.

BELLE HATFIELD PHOTO

And then it was gone

The old poor farm was demolished on Monday.

An article from the Vanguard *newspaper, Yarmouth, March 26, 1997, regarding the demolition of the poor house in Arcadia, Yarmouth County. This poor house was built in 1870, closed in 1972 and demolished in 1997. Special thanks to Lisette Comeau, of the Yarmouth County Museum, for bringing this article to my attention.*

Arcadia Poor House, Yarmouth County

The poor house in Arcadia was another of a handful of poor houses built outside of Halifax prior to the County Incorporation Act of 1879. It was constructed in 1870 and took in paupers and mentally ill persons.[72] In the first report on this institution, in 1889, Dr. Page notes:

> The Yarmouth Township Poor House is situated in a pretty village called Arcadia, on the Chebogue River, between two and three miles from the Town ... The building is much larger than necessary – four stories high – the third and fourth stories very little used.[73]

Dr. Page also writes that there were 27 inmates – 16 males and 11 females – and that the water supply is "poor and uncertain." In 1890, Dr. Page reports that the "house is clean and warm and the diet is excellent" and that "a doctor visits the house once a week. The clergy don't come at all." Dr. Page notes again that the water supply is poor.[74]

By 1891, new poor house keepers had been hired as the previous ones retired. Dr. Page notes that the new keepers "will do well if they sustain the good character of the institution for cleanliness and comfort. They have had painful evidence of some unsanitary surroundings in the death of a bright little son about five years old."[75] This is a rather harsh comment given that the poor keepers were new to the job and the problem with the water existed prior to their arrival.

The next year, 1892, the water situation still had not been improved and Dr. Page now blamed the municipality: "But there are certain matters for which the municipality is responsible, and to which I alluded in last year's report, that are yet without remedy. Chief among these is the poor water supply."[76]

By 1898, however, the water issue had been fixed and Dr. Page notes that, amongst the 24 inmates, six were children, and that "the hot water heating apparatus put in last fall gives satisfaction."[77]

Dr. G.L. Sinclair takes over from Dr. Page as the inspector in 1899 and notes that all is well with the poor house apart from one concern:

> At my first inspection there were some very young children, who were placed in charge of insane women, the matron saying it was impossible

to get any other to care for them. A risky business, I should imagine. The housework is done by the matron, with what aid she can get from the inmates, sane or insane.[78]

The Yarmouth Poor House was used as a model by several other municipalities considering the establishment of their own poor houses, asylums and almshouses. The Senior Scribes write: "The municipal officials in Pictou County ... visited and corresponded with Yarmouth officials before they built the Poor House at Chebogue River in 1896."[79]

Argyle Poor Farm, Yarmouth County

Built in 1902, the Argyle Poor Farm was discontinued as a poor house in the 1960s and closed for good in 1972. It is now used as an apartment building. Photo by author, May 2017.

In May, 1901, after a committee was struck to seek out a place that would be suitable for a poor house, the municipality of Argyle purchased the property of David Forbes. This purchase included a farmhouse and a barn, 320 acres of land, several heads of cattle and shares in a boat. Prior to this purchase, the poor of the area were boarded out to private homes which were selected by the overseer of the poor, and the mentally ill were sent to Mount Hope Mental Hospital in Dartmouth.

Dr. Sinclair visited the almshouse (see definition, p. 56) in 1903 and wrote in his annual report:

> The building occupied by them is quite new and excellently planned, having many single bedrooms, also lavatories, bathrooms, and water closets. The portions occupied by male and female are entirely separated. Each sex has its own dining room ... Among the inmates are seven mentally defective; two of these transfers from the hospital. To prevent

one of them running away mechanical restraint was employed but since my visit has been discontinued.[80]

The Argyle Poor Farm was a much smaller facility than most of the poor farms in the province, at most housing 20 inmates. It continued to act as a Home for Special Care into the 1960s, when most of the poor houses had closed down. The facility was closed for good on November 22, 1972.[81]

Local resident Dianne Crowell used to volunteer at this home with her mother when Dianne was a child and, as a teenager, she ran a youth hostel for one summer in the building. Crowell believes that the barred cells, also called the "strong rooms," in the basement, are still in existence.

Aylesford Poor House, Kings County

In 1891, Aylesford Township opened the doors of its newly established poor house, 6.5 kilometres away in the hamlet of Greenwood.[82] The Senior Scribes tell us that early recording of this poor house also refers to the location as Auburn and Aylesford. In 1891, Inspector Page visited the poor house and wrote in his annual report:

The buildings are old and poorly adapted to the purpose, especially the dormitories, which like those at Greenwich [Horton] are furnished with wooden bedsteads of the plainest and poorest quality, suitable only for a breeding place for vermin ... The clothing is slop made and poor in quality ... No bathroom. No bathing. No fire escapes. No doctor regularly. No religious services.[83]

However, Dr. Page remarks that there is a reason for this poor upkeep:

The excuse given for the objectionable character of the buildings in these three townships [Horton, Auburn, and Cornwallis] is that the county authorities are discussing the propriety of having a county institution, capable of accommodating the chronic insane as well as the poor, and they hesitate before making improvements until a decision is reached by the Municipal Council.

In 1892, Dr. Page writes in his annual report that only five inmates are living there. He notes that the house is "clean and orderly," that "the beds are clean and good," but that "the bedsteads are poor and worthless."[84]

The inmates of the Aylesford poor house were able to work and their work resulted in a profit for the farm. In a scathing tone, Dr. Page writes:

The farm is a good one, and so well managed that last year the poor were well supported and one hundred dollars placed *at rest*. It is probably the only instance on record of paupers laying up money honestly! (emphasis mine)

In 1898, the last year of inspections done by Dr. Page, he notes that there are 20 inmates in the poor farm, "five of whom are insane, the balance are poor, with 2 epileptics, 2 idiotic, and 1 each of violent and filthy."[85]

In 1899, Dr. Sinclair writes about the poor farm:

> The inmates are comfortably clothed and well fed. The house is an ordinary farm house, but it is clean and well kept ... Conversing with the more intelligent, I heard no complaints and all seemed as comfortable and satisfied as could be expected.[86]

In 1926 the County Asylum for the Insane was built in Waterville and this poor house continued to function as a home for people with mental illness until 1972. The old farmhouse used for the Aylesford Poor Farm eventually burned down.

Barrington Poor House, Shelburne County

The Barrington Poor House was established in 1887 when the county warden, J.B. Lawrence, and the county councillors decided to obtain a municipal poor house in order to end the practice of auctioning off the poor. The property of the late Thomas W. Wilson was purchased for $1,500 on what is now known as Crow's Neck Beach.[87] Like the poor people who had been auctioned off, inmates were expected to work for their keep if they were able to do so.

Dr. Page wrote in his annual report of 1891 that the Barrington Poor House should be known as the Banner Poor House for the Province:

> Visited October 21st. The Barrington House, on account of its substantial and inexpensive fire escape, it's well painted floors and its general fitness for accommodation of the small number present, deserves to be called the Banner Poor House of the Province. Not that the management, good as it is, is any better than at many others, but simply for the reasons given above, and those points of excellence are not expensive or difficult to procure.[88]

The reports on this poor house for the following years are all positive. They record a regular inmate population of between 12 and 14, some of whom were epileptic and classified as "insane." By the 1960s, those who were eligible were receiving pensions from the federal government and were able to support themselves outside the home. In 1967, the poor house was re-classified as a home for the disabled.[89]

In 1973, the municipal council began work on the Bay Side Home to replace the old poor house and the new facility was opened in 1975.[90] The old poor house was torn down shortly afterwards. Bay Side Home is now an adult residential centre for people living with mental and physical challenges; its website describes its mandate as providing respect and dignity for all its residents.

Billtown Poor House, Kings County

The Billtown Poor House in King's County, 1925. Photo Courtesy of the private collection of Wayne E. Baltzer.

The poor house in Billtown, also described as the Cornwallis Poor House, was established in 1858, well before the County Incorporation act of 1879. There are no reports from inspections, however, until 1891.

Dr. A.C. Page wrote in his annual report:

Visited September 15th. The Cornwallis Poor Farm is located at Billtown. It is a good farm for the purpose and is well worked...The buildings are very poor. The keeper gets very little help outside and the matron none inside. Very little sickness. No regular Medical supervision. No bath-room. House not heated throughout. No enclosed grounds. No pains taken to keep sexes separate.[91]

In his annual report of 1892, Dr. Page is scathing about the Billtown Poor House in his annual report in which he writes:

This house has been painted outside since my previous visit, which improved its appearance greatly, but no amount of pain will ever make it other than a "Whited Sepulchre."[92]

Dr. Page also notes that there are thirty inmates, which includes six babies; the previous winter the poor house keeper notes that he had 56 inmates[93].

By 1898 the situation has not improved with Dr. Page writing in his annual report:

> Visited June 25th, 1898. Present in June – Males 13; females 15; children, 9; Total 37. None insane, several imbecile, all poor. Epileptic 1; filthy, 2. Deaths during the year, 5...There is a very offensive cesspool for sink water, stands under the window at the rear of the house, which is a menace to the whole household.[94]

By 1922, the poor house in Billtown was amalgamated with the poor houses in Aylesford and Horton into the poor house in Waterville. The inmates from these old poor houses were transferred into the new one in Waterville in November 1922 and the old properties were sold.

Cape Breton County Asylum, Sydney River

The Cape Breton County Asylum was established in 1889 on Kings Road, referred to as Riverside, approximately three miles from the town of Sydney. The large wooden structure was "architecturally ... typical of Victorian era institutions ... very similar to the factories and prisons of the period."[95]

It was not, as such, a poor house so much as an asylum for the mentally ill; however, like most asylums and poor houses of the time, it was a catch-all for most forms of human misery. Officials at the time often associated poverty with mental illness and crime and thus paupers were housed in asylums such as this one.[96]

In 1890, Dr. Page inspected the facility and was disappointed to find so many problems:

> The house needs a thorough overhauling and cleaning. It is still over-crowded ... Likewise there is no place to be used as a mortuary.
> The beds, almost all, are straw sacks, *and as no sheets are in use throughout the house* and the blankets are grey, they do not present an attractive appearance. (emphasis Dr. Page's)[97]

However, he was willing to give some consideration for the newness of the asylum when he wrote in the same report: "This is the first year for the Sydney Asylum and, any shortcomings should be looked upon with a certain degree of allowance."[98]

Inspector Dr. Page visited the asylum a second time that year, on December 15, and writes in the same report that he is disappointed to find the situation unimproved:

> The inmates number thirty-three – sixteen males and seventeen females. None are violent; but four of each sex are filthy, and the bathing facilities are very poor. One (Mr. S) is suicidal ... A noteworthy feature in the house furnishing line is that it is entirely without bedsteads.[99]

By the time Dr. Page did his inspection in 1891, he again noted not a lot of improvements. However, he did meet with the commissioners and "pressed on their notice" the need for several reforms. One of these was for fire escapes. The seventh reform in Dr. Page's list is the following:

The propriety of investigating the case of an old lady whose face and body I found much bruised and discolored, and as there were suspicions that the management was responsible, I deemed it only justice to the keeper that due enquiry should be made in order that, if possible, his innocence should be established and proper steps taken to prevent a recurrence of an event so regrettable.[100]

By 1907, a new hospital was built to replace the old asylum and Dr. Sinclair was enthusiastic about the possibilities for the future. The Senior Scribes note, however, that even though there was a new hospital, the old attitudes towards those in poverty and suffering from mental illness prevailed: In short, the facility was called a hospital but remained an asylum or shelter with little or no active treatment programs for the residents.[101]

The writing group Senior Scribes note that during the First World War, conditions began to deteriorate with overcrowding.[102] It's possible that this could have been due to the general anxiety, stress and depression that accompany wars, not only for the soldiers but also for their families, who are left behind to worry and cope without their sons, husbands and fathers.

Extensions were made to the hospital in 1924 and again in 1940. On March 22, 1950, there was a major fire with, fortunately, no loss of life. However, a new facility was needed as soon as possible. A new hospital was opened in 1955, but there had been so many rumours of abuse of patients and staff dissension during the time it took to build the facility that a Royal Commission of Inquiry was appointed in 1956 to investigate. The result was a number of "sweeping changes," which led to improvements in the treatment of patients. As the Senior Scribes note, this "had the long term effect of changing what was a holding asylum into a modern mental hospital."[103]

Chester Poor House, Lunenburg County

In 1911, the Chester Municipality appointed a committee to investigate the idea of establishing a poor farm within their municipal district. After visiting the poor farm in Dayspring, Lunenburg County, the committee recommended that Chester should open and operate a similar institution.[104] An old farm house was purchased approximately 6.5 kilometers from the town of Chester and a small wing was added to provide accommodation for the poor house keeper and his wife.[105] Prior to the opening of the Chester Poor House, paupers were boarded out within the seven poor districts in the area. In 1923, the first official report on the facility states that there were 13 inmates. The report also notes that the facility had neither bath nor water closet and that, due to its layout and size, separation of the sexes was "difficult."

During the 1920s the population of the Chester Poor House dwindled and by 1928, there was only one inmate.[106] In 1933, the Chester Council was concerned about the cost of upkeep of the poor house, discussing whether they should send their poor to nearby facilities, such as the Dayspring Poor House. By 1936, the council gave the executive council permission to sell the poor farm as the municipality had no further use for it.[107]

Colchester Poor Farm, North River

Colchester Poor Farm, North River, opened in 1908 and burned down in 1954. Photo courtesy of Dr. Allan E. Marble.

The poor and "harmless insane" were cared for in Colchester County in the same manner as in the rest of the province – they were boarded out in private homes to those citizens who charged the county the lowest amount for their care. Once the paupers or "harmless insane" were boarded out, there was very little to no supervision or follow up to check on their health and well-being.[108] This was increasingly seen as an imperfect system, but the citizens did not know what else to do with the "misfits," the aged who needed care, unwed mothers and people who were disabled, addicted or homeless. Colchester County decided that a poor farm, such as were in operation in other parts of the province, would be a solution. It would be "a place to keep our poor, and to humanely care for our harmless insane."[109]

The purchase of a local farm, which consisted of 80 acres of cultivated land and 130 acres of woodland, was approved by council in 1904. The Poor Farm became a reality in 1908. The first inspection of the new facility was made by Dr. Sinclair in September 1908. Although separate buildings for the poor and the "insane" were argued for, finances curtailed the idea and the "harmless insane" and the paupers were put in the same building. The Senior Scribes describe it:

As might be expected, financial pressures and the lack of a separate facility for the long term mentally ill resulted in the Colchester Poor Farm becoming a dumping ground for the mentally retarded and those so-called "quiet" mental patients who were tractable and could be easily cared for in an open institution such as the poor farm.[110]

On September 30, 1954, the Colchester Poor Farm burned to the ground. The fire left over 105 inmates (including six children), the staff and their families homeless. It also took the life of one man. In 1955 the property was purchased by a local family. They cleaned up the burial site in 2001 and put up a monument to those buried on the property.[111]

The county purchased Beech Hill Farms at Princeport in 1955 and moved some of the inmates there. It continued as a home for the aged until 1975.[112]

Cole Harbour Poor Farm, Halifax County

Halifax County Poor Farm in Cole Harbour. The buildings were used to separate men from women. Photo courtesy of Cole Harbour Farm Museum.

In 1886 the Municipality of the County of Halifax purchased the family farm of Harriet Roche on Bissett Road in Cole Harbour.[113] At the time, Cole Harbour was a rural area of farms and forests located 11 kilometres from the town of Dartmouth. In 1887 the Halifax County Poor Farm was established to take some of the overpopulation strain from Mount Hope Asylum for the Insane, located just outside of Dartmouth. Dr. Page notes, in his 1990 Report on Public Charities: "Seventeen have been transferred from Mount Hope, and one admitted as a pauper."[114]

The inmates, who consisted of the poor, the "insane," and their children were expected to do chores, such as farm labour in the fields and buildings to help produce crops and food for the staff and residents. Dr. Page, upon inspecting the poor farm in 1892, makes note: "The farm did very well this year, although the amount of help obtained from the inmates was very small, as you would expect it to be from feeble old men."[115]

The farm consisted of three buildings, 20 x 40 feet, which were "well built."[116] However, in 1891, Dr. Page notes that "the buildings, although on rather spring, wet ground, have no cellars, and are not raised much above the surface, which will involve much dampness of the floors."[117] By 1899, Dr. Sinclair notes:

The inside of the house is in need of repairs at the hands of the painter, plasterer and carpenter. It is much crowded, and I do not think it will be safe to send any more insane patients to the institution till more accommodation is provided. A rough calculation shows that there is not more than 400 cubic feet of air space for each inmate.[118]

Dr. Sinclair states in the same report that there were three children in residence, 10 sane men, 10 sane women, 14 "insane" men, and 13 "insane" women, along with six "imbeciles" and epileptic men and seven "imbeciles" and epileptic women – for a total of 63 people living in this accommodation, in addition to staff.

The Senior Scribes note: "The history of this Poor Farm from 1886 to 1929 was very much like the other poor houses in the province. There was no separate facility for mental patients; they were all housed in one building with the indigent and children."[119]

In 1929, most of the dormitory structures were severely damaged by fire.[120]

In 1916, Dr. W.H. Hattie made reference to the fact that Halifax County was considering the erection of a new facility for the insane; however, it was not until the 1940s that this idea came to fruition.[121] In 1943, although the name of the poor farm was changed to the Halifax County Hospital, the poor and the "insane," along with children with mental disabilities, continued to be housed there.[122]

In 1977, the institution's name changed again, to the Halifax County Rehabilitation Centre and its mandate was to care for patients who had difficulty living on their own in the community.[123] This centre operated until 2002, when it was finally closed.

For a short while, the Nova Scotia-based television show *Trailer Park Boys* used the abandoned buildings of the rehab centre as a set.[124] In 2010, the provincial government approved the demolition of the rehab centre, but before this could be carried out, one of the buildings was damaged by fire, presumed to be the result of arson. Much of the fire was contained to a separate building at the back.[125]

In 2016, Halifax Regional Council voted to turn the former poor farm and rehab lands into parkland.[126]

Cumberland County Asylum, Pugwash

The facility at Pugwash was much delayed and fought over. Originally, there were no specialized services offered for either the poor or the "insane" in the area.[127] In 1882, a committee from the county visited the Mount Hope Asylum, near Dartmouth, with the idea of gathering information about the needs of the Cumberland County patients who were housed in this hospital. The committee concluded that mentally ill patients could not be housed alongside the poor as they required one-on-one care and separate accommodations.[128]

The Cumberland County Council was warned several times by the Mount Hope Asylum and the Commissioner of Mines and Works that they would have to provide accommodation and help for their own "insane" citizens as there were too many from Cumberland County in Mount Hope. In 1892, a mentally ill patient was being held in the Amherst jail, with two doctors having certified him as insane. An application was made for his removal to Mount Hope but the superintendent there refused to admit the Cumberland patient because the Asylum was overcrowded and because Cumberland had not taken any steps to establish their own facility. As a result, the patient being held in the Amherst jail was sent home.[129] Finally, in 1893, Cumberland Council appointed a committee of five to select an appropriate site upon which to build an asylum. In the spring of that year the farm of James N. Benjamin was purchased for use as a home for the "harmless insane." The following year a motion was passed to build an alms-house (see definition, p.50) at this site. However, as was the case in much of the province, the county councillors considered the problems of caring for the poor and the mentally ill as a single issue and saw no need for separate facilities.[130]

Dr. Sinclair inspected the institution in 1899, referring to it as the Cumberland County Asylum. He notes that the patients were well looked after and the house was clean from cellar to attic. There were 55 inmates in the facility at the time, with only one labelled as "sane."[131]

In 1907, the Poor Committee chair Joseph Turner stated: "I found that there are people who would suffer rather than apply for assistance, while there are others that are a little jealous about getting their rightful share of the funds in charge of the poor committee." He also thought that the county should be coming up with a plan for a separate poor house as he did not think it was right that the poor must stay in the same building as the insane.[132]

In 1950, the Province of Nova Scotia took on the financial responsibility of caring for the mentally ill in certain municipal facilities, with the Pugwash asylum being one of them. In 1976, the name was changed to the Sunset Adult Residential Centre and admission is now restricted to adults with mental challenges who have difficulty living in their communities.[133]

Digby Municipal Poor House, Marshalltown

Marshalltown Almshouse, outside of Digby, was built in the 1930s after the Poor Farm in Marshalltown was closed. Note the child in the foreground. By this time, children were not supposed to be kept in poor houses but sent to orphanges. Circumstances, however, such as lack of transportation and overcrowding at orphanages often meant that children stayed at poor houses. Image courtesy of The Marshalltown Almshouse Voices for Hope Facebook Group.

After the death of Charlotte Hill and the resulting hanging of Joe Tibo, the Enquiry into the Poor of Digby examined the idea that a poor house may be a solution for the poor of the area. The municipal government did establish a poor farm but there seems to be some confusion about where and when the poor farm was opened. The Digby Municipal Council decided, after hearing favourable reports from other counties with poor houses, to open their own poor house. A committee was established to find land and accommodation and the farm of Robert Marshall of Marshalltown was purchased in 1890. 25 acres of land came with the purchase.

Here is where the confusion began: an area politician, Victor Cardoza, stated that the Poor House was built in 1891 and opened for inmates in 1892. Later historians, writers and researchers repeated this error. In fact, the iconic building called the Marshalltown Almshouse (see definition below), located on the former farmland of Robert Marshall, was not built until the 1930s. I learned this in conversation with a Marshalltown woman whose mother was born in the original poor farm and moved to the new asylum in the 1930s. Robert Marshall's house and farm were used for several years as the area poor farm. This is confirmed in the Public Charities Report of 1892:

> The Digby County Poor Farm is a new institution. It has only been in operation one year, and the house is already quite full ... It is located in Marshalltown, on high and dry grounds, and I should think a very healthy spot. The old buildings, with some additions and alterations are being utilized for the present.[134]

In 1900, Dr. Sinclair also attests to the use of the old farm buildings in his report:

> The house is an old, very old, farmhouse, and has outlived its usefulness. I say this, because it is the intention of the Municipality to erect this year a more commodious asylum especially adapted to the particular purpose to which it will be devoted.[135]

Dr. Sinclair notes in his report in 1899 that there was no municipal hospital for the "harmless insane" in Digby, so most of them ended up living at the Poor Farm.

The poor farm was indeed opened to the poor people of the area in 1892, but it was not the iconic building that came to be known as the area poor house. The almshouse of the 1930s was a wooden structure built in the neo-Georgian style that made a revival in the early 20th century. The Marshalltown asylum was the only poor house in the province to be called an "almshouse." Traditionally, a poor house was tax-supported, while an almshouse was supported by the local church. We can only guess at the reason for the official label of the facility in Marshalltown; perhaps the organizers thought almshouse sounded more dignified than poor house.

Maud Lewis. Image courtesy of Martha Woolaver.

In 2017, an archeological study was done in preparation for the twinning of Highway 101 through Marshalltown. The researchers found two foundations and two unmarked graveyards, one on the land that had been occupied by the almshouse and another north of there, at the site of the former Robert Marshall farm.[136]

Everett Lewis, husband of famous folk artist Maud Lewis, spent time as a young child at the poor farm. His father and some of his siblings died there. His mother managed to get herself and Everett out of the poor house. Everett eventually became a day labourer, fish peddler and anything else that would earn him an income. He married Maud in 1938 and they lived in a very small house just down the road from the Marshalltown Almshouse. Eventually he became the night watchman for the almshouse, where his brother still lived.

I recommend *Maud Lewis: Heart on the Door*, Lance Woolaver's comprehensive book about Everett and Maud and the Marshalltown Almshouse. It was closed in 1963 and burned down in an act of arson in 1995. (see also front cover)

Article from the Digby Courier, *July 25, 2001. An area resident points out where the unmarked graves of the Marshalltown Poor Farm and Almshouse are located.*

Halifax Poor House

Concrete sewer blocks made by inmates of the poor house, outside the Halifax Poor House, corner of Robie and Inglis streets. Photo courtesy of Dr. Alan Marble.

The grandparent of all poor houses in Nova Scotia, the Halifax Poor House, built in 1750, was the first one in the province. It was located on the site of what is now Government House, 1451 Barrington Street. Halifax was much smaller in those early days and that site was considered outside of the town. As was usual then, the outskirts were deemed appropriate for locating an asylum for sick soldiers and the "miscreants of the town."[137]

The Lords of Trade in London were not happy with the expenditure for this building and Governor Cornwallis was pressed to explain why the arriving settlers could not pay for their own medical expenses and support.[138] The fact that thousands of settlers were arriving on ships that had travelled for weeks and months would explain much of the illness. In addition, the new town of Halifax was growing rapidly and there was not enough housing for everyone. Many new residents spent the first harsh winters and cold springs in tents, resulting in much disease and many deaths.[139]

In 1759, an Act for Relief of the Poor was passed and the Office of the Overseer of the Poor was created. By 1760, a new combination poor house and work house was in the process of being erected at the corner of Spring Garden

Road and Queen Street.[140] Again, this was outside of the town. Local resident Jonathan Harris was appointed the keeper of the work house in 1760 and, as the original civic hospital and almshouse were closed, the work house became the only institution to receive the sick and poor.[141]

"Grateful for the Applause and Patronage which he has obtained since his stay in the Town, has the pleasure to inform the ladies and gentlemen, that he will give the presentation for the BENEFIT OF THE POOR and this brilliant representation, Mr. Brunell illustrates himself in merit the same applause he has heretofore received."

Additions were made to the poor house/ work house over the years to accommodate the growing numbers of persons who were sick, poor and abandoned. Many people from other countries ended up in Halifax, seeking to escape desperate situations at home. The Senior Scribes write: "Into this supposedly wealthy urban area came hordes of human beings seeking employment or merely escaping from hopeless situations elsewhere. From Ireland, Great Britain, the United States and other Atlantic colonies they came."[142]

For many years the poor, the mentally ill,

Advertisement for a presentation for the benefit of the poor given by Boston Resident, Mr. Brunell. Acadian Recorder, Halifax, September 25, 1819 p. 3.

orphaned children and those who had committed petty crimes were grouped together into this institution despite repeated requests for separate facilities.[143] Finally, in 1858, a "lunatic asylum" (now known as the Nova Scotia Hospital) for the "hopeless insane" was opened at Mount Hope, on the Dartmouth side of the harbour. The City Hospital, which eventually came to be known as the Victoria General Hospital, was opened for the sick the following year.[144] This took some of the pressure off the crowded conditions at the poor house.

In 1869, a new poor house was built at the corner of South and Robie Streets, where the Izaak Walton Killam Children's Hospital is today. This new poor house was one of the largest buildings in the province and could easily house 600 people. The belief that the sick poor would be best served by being on the top floor of the institution, to have the freshest air possible, was good in its intention but disastrous when the fire of 1882 levelled the building. The elevators did not reach the top floor where the bedridden and disabled paupers were located and many could not make it down the stairs. Therefore, many of them perished in the fire. The survivors of the fire were housed in jails, camps and churches until a new poor house was built on the same site in 1886.[145]

The reports by inspectors Page and Sinclair are favourable following the re-build. In 1890, Dr. Page notes that there were 285 inmates in the facility, of which 100 were "insane" and one was a child. He also writes: "It would only be a repetition of former reports to say that everything about this institution, so far as cleanliness, care, diet and good order are concerned, is without fault."[146]

By 1901, however, the building was said to be at its limit with residents, especially in the winter as poor people were seeking shelter from the weather. This poor house became known as the Halifax City Home by the time it was damaged in the tragic Halifax Explosion of December 6, 1917. The windows were shattered and a great deal of damage was done to the walls. However, the home served to house many of the victims of that explosion.[147]

In 1955, the mayor of Halifax, Leonard Kitz, declared the home to be "hopelessly inadequate." The inspector of humane institutions also made complaints about the home in his reports because of the mixing of "sane" and "insane" people in the same building. In 1958, some of the patients in the Halifax City Home were moved to a new institution at the north end of Gottingen Street. In 1971, other patients were transferred from the Halifax City Home to the new Abbie Lane Memorial Hospital, which is now a part of the Queen Elizabeth ll hospital complex within the Nova Scotia Health Authority.148 The Halifax City Home was eventually demolished to make room for the IWK Children's Hospital.

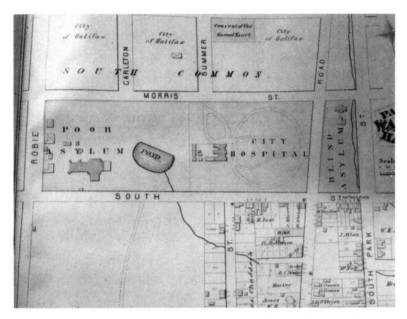

The grounds of the Halifax Poor House on the Corner of South and Robie as shown in the book The City Atlas of Halifax, Nova Scotia 1878. *Photo courtesy of J.W. Doull bookstore.*

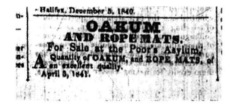

An advertisement for sale of the products made by inmates of the Halifax Poor House.
Acadian Recorder, *December 5, 1840.*

Hants East Municipal Home, South Maitland

The Hants East Municipal Home in South Maitland was also known as the Poor Farm and the County Home in its time.[149] Records indicate that a farm and residence of the late Squire McDougall was purchased by the East Hants Council for the purpose of a home for the poor. The home began operation in 1895, with Dr. Page writing about the home in his report presented to the provincial House of Assembly in 1896:

> The house is a large two storey one, with an ell, and with the contemplated additions and changes, will be very well suited to the purpose. The situation is high and dry, with a very pleasant outlook and surroundings ... the inmates at the time of my visit were 5 old men, 1 old lady and two young children. With one exception, the men are too old and feeble to help on the farm, and the old lady being 76, is no help in the house.[150]

In 1898 Dr. Page notes that there were "10 men, 7 women and 3 children; of whom 7 are "insane" and the balance poor."[151]

The Senior Scribes make a point that the inmates had, for the most part, a serious illness — physical, mental or both. "The common bond among them was the need for care."[152]

After the Second World War, many veterans of the Navy, Army and Air Force were admitted to the home, no doubt suffering from a combination of physical injuries and post traumatic stress disorder, which was called "shell shock" at the time. By 1944, a three storey addition had been attached to the main house. Residents slept dormitory style.[153]

On December 21, 1971, the facility, which had been renamed the Hillside Residence, was closed. The county held an auction in January 1972 and sold off the land, buildings, equipment and other contents.

Horton Poor House, Kings County

Horton Poor House, Kings' County, date unknown. Photo from the private collection of Wayne E. Baltzer.

The Horton Poor House, (also called Greenwich Poor House) opened in Greenwich in 1822, was one of several poor houses that were established before the County Incorporation Act of 1879. The Senior Scribes write that the first overseers of the poor were appointed in 1765. In 1777, the overseers of the poor in Kings County requested money to support the wife and children of Elijah Bent, who had deserted them. As was the case elsewhere in Nova Scotia, prior to the opening of the poor house, the Kings County poor were boarded out with people who hoped to make a profit from their work.[154]

In his inspection report for 1891, Dr. Page writes:

> The Horton farm is very prettily situated in Greenwich, and is a very suitable one, but the house is old and not well adapted to the purpose, being too small and having very poor sleeping accommodations … There are twenty-two inmates, seven of whom are children.[155]

Dr. Page notes that there are no bathing or toilet facilities and no effort to keep the men and women apart. He does report, however, that the theological students from nearby Acadia University minister to the inmates' "spiritual wants every Sabbath – a service which seems highly appreciated."

The next year, 1892, Dr. Page brings attention again to the age and state of the house:

> The house itself is generally dilapidated and not suitable for the purpose. The rooms are clean and comfortable looking, but small and poorly ventilated ... The inmates number nineteen including the six children.[156]

Dr. Page also notes that the matron of the poor house had seven children of her own to care for in addition to the six children that were inmates of the poor house.

On June 17, 1893, the old house was destroyed by fire. Dr. Page, upon visiting the area, wrote:

> I visited the Horton poor in a temporary residence – an old farm house near their late home, which was destroyed by fire on the 17th of June last. The fire was caused by an idiotic inmate and involved no loss of human life.[157]

Some of the inmates were housed in an adjacent barn until a new house could be built.[158] The new house for the poor was built between 1893 and 1894 and the new inspector, Dr. Sinclair, makes note in his 1899 annual report: "This is a large, comparatively new house, well kept and comfortable." At that time there were twenty inmates, five of whom were children.[159]

The Horton Poor House was abandoned in 1922 when Kings County amalgamated the three poor houses in the county into one at Waterville.[160] The poor house was used for many years as an apartment building until it burned down in 1981. It was demolished a few years later and has since been used for building lots.[161]

Lunenburg County Poor Farm and Asylum, Dayspring

Lunenburg County Poor Farm and Asylum, Dayspring, which opened in 1889 and closed in 1980. Photo courtesy of Dr. Allan E. Marble.

Prior to a poor house being set up in Dayspring, the Lunenburg County paupers were "boarded out" amongst "good families" in the area who hoped to make a profit off the sale of the paupers' labour. However, by 1888, E.D. Davison and Sons had presented the county with the "Robar property" at Summerville in Upper LaHave as a gift with the condition of establishing a poor farm there.[162]

The location of the poor farm is now known as Dayspring, which is a few kilometres outside of Bridgewater. In January 1888, the paupers of the area were finally gathered in one location. The regulations that governed this new poor house are interesting, particularly section 5:

That all paupers receiving aid from the municipality shall be placed in the Institution and those who refuse to go shall receive no alms except those who are bedridden and not in a condition to be removed in safety to such Institution.[163]

Dr. Page writes following his first inspection of the facility:

Lunenburg County Poor House was built in 1888 on a 28 acre lot, five acres of it under cultivation. It is pleasantly situated at Summerville, overlooking the beautiful LaHave River. It was built for the poor only, but the buildings are well arranged, and with very little additional expense could be made to accommodate the "quiet insane" for the whole County.[164]

By the next year, 1890, Dr. Page writes in his annual report:

The Lunenburg Poor house contains thirty-four inmates, including three children...the House is much crowded on the females' side.... No bathrooms. No bathing for the men, and no laundry.[165]

In 1891 Dr. Page notes that the Lunenburg Poor house "was visited during the past year with a very severe epidemic of LaGrippe [influenza], which was fatal to twelve of the old people," and that the female side of the house was so crowded that women were sleeping on the male side of the house.[166] In 1898, Dr. Page notes that a building was about to be built to relieve the overcrowding.[167]

Dr. Sinclair, in his 1899 report on Public Charities, calls the facility the Lunenburg County Asylum and Poor Farm. He notes: "A large addition to the original structure was rapidly nearing completion at the time of my last visit ... it is intended mainly as an infirmary for women patients and is arranged accordingly."[168]

By 1903, the number of "insane" inmates had increased dramatically and some form of segregation became an urgent matter. In 1917, a new wing was built that was specifically for the purpose of separation of the sane from the insane.[169]

Eventually the facility became one of six municipally-operated institutions approved by the Provincial Government to care for mentally ill patients within its catchment area of the county. By the 1960s and 1970s, the mentally ill patients at Dayspring were transferred to other facilities and the new programs of senior care took its place. The Senior Scribes write: "On October 31, 1980, the Dayspring Poor Farm and the buildings that were part of it were demolished, and LaHave Manor, a modern nursing home, was built near the site."[170]

In 2015, LaHave Manor rebranded itself as Riverview Enhanced Living, with the goal of being more responsive to the different challenges and demands made upon their services.[171]

Mabou Poor House and Asylum, Inverness County

Mabou Poor House, Inverness County. Date unknown. Photo courtesy of Chestico Museum.

The first inspection report for the asylum in Inverness County shows up in the Legislative records in 1890:

> Mabou has thirty-two inmates. Thirty-eight were admitted, but three have died; two were discharged cured, and one was transferred to Antigonish. None very violent or filthy ... Considerable help is derived from the patients both outdoors and in ... No appliances for use in case of fire. No fire escapes yet.[172]

In 1891, Dr. Page notes with concern that "the inmates number thirty-eight of whom two are violent and two filthy ... The heating system is by stoves and is decidedly condemned by the commissioners and the keeper."[173]

By 1898, Dr. Page notes that the number of inmates has increased dramatically:

Inmates – Male, 51; female, 48; total 99

Poor male, 2; female, 0

.... Idiotic male, 3; female, 2

Violent male, 4; female, 6
Filthy male, 4; female, 6
Deaths, male, 2; female, 0174

In the same report, Dr. Page also states that the heating situation has still not been dealt with despite the condemnation made of this situation seven years earlier: "This house is heated with coal stoves, and the walls and ceilings have got very black."

By 1900, Dr. Sinclair is the new inspector. He reports 96 inmates living in the building, of which 47 are "insane" males and 44 are "insane" females. He notes that the asylum receives cases from Inverness, Victoria and Richmond Counties, which probably is the reason for the large number of inmates in the house. Like Dr. Page, he also comments on the heating situation: "The system of heating by base burner stoves in the halls must be unsatisfactory, if it is not positively dangerous ... There is so much to praise in this asylum that it is all the more regrettable that attention has to be drawn to this sin of commission."[175]

The Senior Scribes recount an interview with a former staff member at the Mabou asylum who worked there in the early 1920s when she was just 15 years old. The person who interviewed her, A.A. MacKenzie, provides her words:

That staff had the same food as the inmates ... They and we slept on mattresses that were kept filled with straw. There were many people between 40 and 60 years of age and some teenagers ... Some of the inmates ran away, escaping on sheets through a chute from the laundry room in the basement.[176]

In another interview, a worker who was there between 1929 and 1935 states:

Food was alright, both our food and what the patients got. There was a lot of porridge and molasses ... There was no recreation! Letters were censored if a patient wrote a letter to go outside ... Patients might get beaten – get a going over sometimes. The women in charge could be pretty rough. Two patients burned to death when the asylum burned. They were located in the basement laundry.[177]

A new asylum had opened in 1924 in Mabou but it burned to the ground on February 4, 1947.[178] The surviving patients were moved to the Mulgrave army barracks, which in 1959 housed 109 patients. By 1961 the barracks closed and patients were either removed to other institutions in the province or returned to their communities, with and without adequate supervision.[179]

Meteghan Poor House, Digby County (a.k.a. St. Mary's Poor House)

St. Mary's Poor House in Meteghan, District of Clare. This was one in a series of postcards of Nova Scotia poor houses. Photo courtesy of anonymous donor.

Two incidents in Digby County would have been responsible for the District of Clare developing a poor house of its own. One was the enactment in 1879 of the County Incorporation Act, which made each county responsible for its own poor. The other incident was the death of Charlotte Hill. As Clare was not far down the road from North Range and the private poor house of poor master Joe Tibo, Charlotte's death would have had a significant impact on the people of this area.

The District of Clare is mainly Acadian and French speaking, and it is geographically distinct from the Loyalist-based, English-speaking Digby Municipality. When Digby County decided upon Marshalltown as the location for its poor house, there was outrage in other areas in the municipality. Some residents felt there was no need for a poor house and the accompanying costs. Others, especially those in the more distant communities on Digby Neck Islands, were concerned with travelling 40 kilometres over rough dirt roads that were barely passable during certain times of the year, to get to the poor house in Marshalltown. In Clare, the problem was the language barrier.

Clare Council met in May 1888 and agreed to appoint a committee to research local land and buildings with a view to establishing a poor house for the area.[180] Marc V. Comeau had offered his place in Meteghan for sale. It had 30 acres on the south side of the Post road and offered a "splendid view and good location not far from church and school, and a resident doctor."[181] In 1896 the two man committee finally submitted a report with information about several poor houses around the province, showing their localities and costs.

We know that the Meteghan Poor House, in the District of Clare in the County of Digby, was built and operating by 1898, as Inspector A.C. Page visited the new institution on June 21 of that year for the first time. Dr. Page proclaimed the Meteghan Poor House to be one of the best in the province.[182]

Dr. Sinclair succeeded Dr. Page in 1899 and he also found the facility to be one of the best asylums in the province. The fact that it was located near the centre of the community it served probably helped it to be a well run facility, as services such as the church, school and doctor for the poor were close by.

The farm that was attached to the poor house had ceased being active by 1947, and the facility itself was closed in 1975.[183]

North Sydney Poor House

The North Sydney Poor House was in existence by 1898, when Dr. Page visited it for the purpose of inspection, and probably earlier as he writes: "The North Sydney Poor House has had but two inmates for years."[184]

In 1899 the North Sydney Poor Asylum is described by Dr. Sinclair:

> The house is an ordinary dwelling, and the inmates all live together as a family. It is heated by grates, has water from a well, and is comfortable and apparently satisfactory to its occupants ... It is as clean as can be expected; the diet is plain, but sufficient, and I heard no complaints.[185]

In 1908 and still by 1911, there was only one inmate. The last report was made by Dr. W.H. Hattie in 1914, when there were two inmates. Dr. Hattie was critical of the condition of the house and "general neglect." The reports stopped after that and, as the Senior Scribes surmise, "one must assume this facility closed sometime around the beginning of the First World War."[186]

Pictou County Poor House, Riverton

Pictou County Poor House, Riverton, opened in 1886 and closed in 1978. Photo courtesy of Dr. Allan E. Marble.

In 1883, 50 mentally ill patients from Pictou County were sent to Mount Hope Hospital, which had been established in Dartmouth in 1858. However, Mount Hope had become hopelessly overcrowded and its superintendent kept pressure on the municipalities to take care of their own "harmless insane" within their own areas. The Pictou County Council examined ways in which they could to this; however, watching the fallout from the Digby County enquiry into the care of their poor and mentally ill and hearing of the abuse that had taken place, the council decided that a poor farm would be a safer and less expensive method than boarding them out.[187]

The Pictou County Poor Farm and Asylum, located in Riverton, was known by many names over the years: the Asylum, the Poor House, the Pictou County Asylum for the Harmlessly Insane, the Pictou County Home and Hospital and the Home for the Disabled.[188]

The annual inspections on the home began shortly after it opened, in 1886. In 1890, Dr. Page reports that there were 65 inmates in the home and that a contract for fire escapes was in the works.[189] By 1891, the fire escapes, consisting of iron stairs attached to the end of the buildings, were in place.[190] In that year, Dr. Page notes that there were 83 inmates, nine of whom died during the year, "mostly old and infirm" but there had been the one case of suicide where the inmate had not shown suicidal tendencies previously.

In 1892, Dr. Page reiterates his concerns about the quality of water in the facility:

> At the time of my visit they had two cases of typhoid fever convalescing. The doctor attributed them to bad water – a very natural conclusion – considering the only supply was from a well, which on account of drought, was at the time almost dry. I have often reported the unsatisfactory water supply here: but the remedy seemed hard to reach."[191]

In 1898, Dr. Page is still noting "Water supply poor" but otherwise praises the management and food of the institution.[192]

In 1922, the poor and the "insane" were no longer housed together in this facility. Pictou County Council decided to build a separate facility for people with mental illness on the same site and the "harmless insane inmates" were moved there. This became known as the Pictou County Hospital for the Mentally Ill. The old poor house became mainly a home for the caring for the aged. A new wing was added in the 1940s.[193]

The year 1965 saw the Towns of New Glasgow, Stellarton, Trenton and Westville following the lead of the Annapolis County Council in opening their own nursing home for the aged. Eventually the old poor house was demolished and a nursing home, Valley View Villa, was built on the same site, opening its doors on January 6, 1978.

Today the facility is known as the Riverview Home, which provides community-based services for individuals with intellectual disabilities, brain injuries and long term mental illness.[194]

CIRCULAR.

County Asylum, Stellarton, N. S. 25th June 1886.

I am instructed to receive Paupers into the Asylum from the Poor Districts in Pictou County, on the following terms.

For Children from 4 to 12 years of age 75 cents to $1.25 per week for Board and Lodging.

For Persons over 12 years of age, $1.00 to $1 50 per week for Board and Lodging.

Clothing, if required, will be furnished at cost.

After the 15th July, the Asylum will be in readiness to take 2 Paupers from each Poor District and three from each of the towns.

The expense of keeping paupers in this Institution is payable by the Overseers of Poor, Quarterly.

Forms of admisssion, to be signed by the Overseers, or Secretary, or Treasurer, are sent herewith.

Overseers intending to send poor to the Asylum will please notify me as soon as possible, giving names and particulars.

JOHN F. MORROW, Keeper.

Stellarton, 25th June 1886.

The contract for Poor Keeper John F. Morrow for the Poor Districts of Pictou County, signed in Stellarton, 1880. Photo courtesy of Riverview Home.

Pictou Town Poor House

In 1886, the Town of Pictou began to operate what was referred to as a poor house, an asylum, a county home and whatever else the inspectors called it in their annual inspection reports. The poor house, however, became overcrowded with paupers and "harmless insane" from the town and the county. By 1895, the County Council of Pictou had issued an ultimatum to the Town of Pictou to take care of their own poor. Accordingly, the town purchased the Lewis Hamblin property on the west side of the Town of Pictou. The building was enlarged and in September 1895, six paupers were transferred from the Truro poor house to the new poor house in the Town of Pictou.[195]

Dr. Page wrote in his annual report in 1898:

Males, 6; females, 6; total 12. Two are children. Water supply good; bathing irregular. House clean. Beds, bedding and clothing good. No sickness. 1 death.[196]

In 1899, the new inspector, Dr. Sinclair, wrote of the Town of Pictou Poor House:

The house is an ordinary dwelling, altered for the present purpose. It is clean, comfortably furnished and satisfactory. *Water is hauled from the town in puncheons.* (emphasis Dr. Sinclair's)[197]

In his report of 1903, Dr. Sinclair reports there were 10 inmates – six males and four females. By 1908 the population had been reduced to four men and one woman. By the end of the year 1920, there was only one patient (the term had been changed from inmate to patient by this time) in care at the poor house.[198]

Queens County Poor Farm and Asylum, Middlefield

It took Queens County some time to set up its poor house as the debate as to which system was better for the poor – a poor house or auctioning the poor – continued for nearly a hundred years. By 1892, the Queens County Municipal Council was facing bills of more than $4,400 annually to the Mount Hope Asylum in Dartmouth for housing the county's insane. This seemed to shock the council into taking action and in 1893 a poor farm was established at Middlefield, a community between Annapolis Royal and Liverpool.[199]

In his report of 1898, Dr. Page notes that the house was not suitable:

The buildings being made of wood and the new part being ceiled instead of plastered, heated with wood stoves, makes the whole thing simply a tinder box, which will require constant vigilance on the part of those in charge.[200]

Dr. Sinclair, in his report the next year, writes of the same concerns:

This asylum is, architecturally, not well designed for caring for the sane and insane, under one roof ... there are ten sleeping rooms, five on either side, upon each floor. The partitions are tongued and grooved wood, the bedsteads also are of wood, and it has so far proved impossible to keep either the beds or the partitions free from vermin ... the whole place is very vulnerable, and has been described as a "fire-trap"[201]

Dr. Sinclair was also upset about the violent and "insane" inmates who were housed in this asylum:

Briefly I advised ... the sending to the Hospital for the Insane of a young woman patient, a recent case, who should never have been admitted to the asylum at all, and, at least, of one man, who, from violence was unmanageable, and at the time of my visit was, and had for some time been *handcuffed and locked in a strong room*. (emphasis Dr. Sinclair's)

The Senior Scribes list the by-laws for the management of the Queen's County Poor House:

- No liquor allowed
- No smoking without the permission of the Keeper or Matron
- No inmate allowed to leave the premises without a written order from the Clerk of the Overseers of the Poor
- All inmates who are able shall be set to work after breakfast[202]

Dr. Sinclair speculates as to why the establishment was located where it was:

The location of this house puts it beyond the reach of many people who otherwise could visit it and see as to its management. It is fourteen miles from everywhere, and the road leading to it is bad. If it is advantageous to have it placed in about the centre of the county, I know of no other reason to justify its isolated and retired position.[203]

In 1927, an addition was built on to the poor farm to house the "insane," who were previously kept in Mount Hope hospital in Dartmouth. The county councillors were not happy with the amount that Mount Hope charged, which was more than a poor house would. All the same, in the poor farm, poor people, children and the mentally ill were all housed together and this was felt to be no longer acceptable.[204]

Eventually the facility was changed to house the elderly and became known as Hillsview Acres. The Senior Scribes tell us that the stigma associated with this house carried well into the 20th century, to the extent that the people of Middlefield would not allow anyone from the poor house to be buried in the community cemetery right across the road. The unclaimed bodies of those who died in the poor house in Middlefield are buried in unmarked graves along the stone walls surrounding the property.[205]

The rock wall that surrounds the former Middlefield Poor House in Queens County. The dead of the poor house are recorded as being buried along the rock wall. Photo by author July 2017.

Richmond County Poor House, St. Peters

The Richmond County Poor House lasted less than 10 years. In 1912, Dr. Sinclair makes note in his Report on Public Charities that the Richmond County Asylum, located just over three miles from the village of St. Peters, was the latest addition to the asylums of the province. He describes the house as a "gloomy wooden building with inadequate heating, insufficient water supply and no proper fire escapes."[206] Like other poor houses and asylums of the day, the children, poor people and those with mental illnesses were housed together under one roof.

Dr. W.H. Hattie followed Dr. Sinclair as the inspector of the poor houses and asylums. In his 1914 report he notes that the water supply was so inadequate that the toilets could only be flushed occasionally, and the bedding was unclean.[207]

On December 22, 1920, a fire destroyed this facility. There were 28 inmates housed there at the time and they were transferred to the Nova Scotia Hospital and other poor houses in neighbouring counties. This poor house was never rebuilt.[208]

Shelburne Municipal Poor House

*Shelburne County Asylum and Poor Farm, opened in 1885
and closed in 1958. Photo courtesy of Dr. Allan E. Marble.*

The Town of Shelburne was a Loyalist landing spot at the end of the American Revolution. A poor house was established at this point, but after the Loyalist refugee years were over and Shelburne's population quickly diminished, the town moved from housing their poor in a poor house to recommending that "the poor which are or may become chargeable to the Township may be publicly sold to the lowest Bidder for their support, provided they are in a state to be removed." In 1806 the Overseers of the Poor proposed that all the town's paupers be gathered and put into some place altogether by themselves, as the poor house was not in a condition to receive them.[209]

The Senior Scribes write that the County Incorporation Act of 1879 and the decline in shipbuilding led to renewed calls for improving the care of paupers of the area.[210] The new poor house was opened on October 21, 1885 and was located just over three miles from the Town of Shelburne on a piece of land overlooking the town.

In his report of 1889, Dr. Page writes:

Between one and two miles from the Town, facing the harbour, in a very pretty and retired spot, is situated the lofty and imposing structure erected for a home for the poor and insane of Shelburne County.[211]

In the same report, he notes that there is "no protection from fire, except two good ladders kept in the cellar," and that the inmates help out with the maintenance of the farm "a good deal inside and out." In 1890, Dr. Page states that the farm is expanding and improving and that, of the 12 inmates, four are "insane" and one man is "treacherous, cross and troublesome", while one of the "insane" women "has periodic fits of violent mania, when she is dangerous and destructive."[212]

By 1898, Dr. Page writes that there are 24 inmates living in the poor house, of which one was epileptic, one was idiotic, two were filthy and all were poor. Two deaths occurred during the year. Dr. Page also notes that the inmates are all either very old or very young and, consequently, cannot help out much at the facility.[213]

Dr. Sinclair's report of 1899 states that there is only one fire extinguisher and, as the house is lofty, there should be an outside fire escape. Of the 24 inmates housed there, five were children and two adults were classed as "insane." Dr. Sinclair "saw and spoke with all the inmates who seemed to be satisfied with the care bestowed upon them."[214]

The home was destroyed by fire in 1913, with Dr. Sinclair noting in his annual report that the fire was caused by a "defective flue" and that "all the inmates, more than 30, were removed to safety, the defectives lodged temporarily in the Jail and the others in buildings and tents." The following year Dr. Sinclair reported that the patients were being temporarily housed in an old farm building until a new building could be erected.[215]

The Shelburne Poor House was closed in the 1950s and was replaced by a non-profit nursing home, Roseway Manor, in 1974. The old poor house was demolished and the Sandy Point Consolidated Elementary School was built on the site.

Sydney Mines Poor House

The poor house in Sydney Mines was a small house. Dr. Page visited this facility in 1895 and describes it as "an ordinary miner's dwelling" that was in need of repair as it was in poor shape.[216] At that time only three adult females were housed there. By 1897 only two elderly women lived there, and the house was still in poor condition and in need of repair.[217]

In 1898 Dr. Page writes:

> There are but 3 inmates, 1 male and 2 females, all old and feeble. They are well fed, but their clothing is poor. The house is open to the wind and they are asking for paper to put over the cracks. They complain that the overseers never come to see how they fare, or what they need.[218]

In 1899, Dr. Sinclair recounts the concerns of the three inmates in the house, a man and two women: "There are no visitors of any kind, and one of the old people complained of this, and said the house was very cold in winter."[219] By 1902, Dr. Sinclair reports that the Sydney Mines facility had closed.[220]

Truro Poor House

The Truro Poor House was located on Willow Street and was established at least by 1897, as Dr. Page visited there on April 5 of that year. Willow Street was at that time outside of the town of Truro, but Dr. Page notes that "it is sufficiently near the town to have the benefit of the Fire Department." Dr. Page describes the house as being "attractive in appearance and nicely located," with 22 acres of land and a woodlot of 50 acres. He refers to the transient poor as the "tramp nuisance":

> This house must be found a very convenient way of disposing of the tramp nuisance, for, since the opening in November, no less than fifty of that class have been lodged and fed there, some of them stopping two days, waiting I suppose, for the weather to clear up, and fit to resume their journey.[221]

In 1900, Dr. Sinclair describes the Truro Poor House as follows:

> It is a new building, erected by the town especially for its own poor ... there were only nine inmates, yet so poorly arranged is the house for its particular purpose, that it seemed full. I find all the inmates are sleeping on the same floor almost "vis-a-vis" and all bedroom doors are left unlocked at night. I suggested a rearrangement of quarters by which the sexes should occupy different floors ... The attic is used as a place for tramps to sleep in. It is unfinished and a very vulnerable part of the house to fire.[222]

By 1927, Dr. A.C. Jost was the Inspector of Humane Institutions and reports that there were three males and seven females in the Truro Poor House. The 1928 annual report on Humane Institutions indicated there were no inmates at the Truro Poor House and it is assumed it was closed by the end of the fiscal year of September 30, 1928.[223]

Waterville Poor House, Kings County

*Waterville Poor House, opened in 1922 as the Kings' County poor houses merged
into one facility. Photo courtesy of Randy Rockwell.*

The Waterville Poor House opened in 1922 as a result of the merging of
operations from the poor houses in Billtown, Aylesford and Horton. The Senior
Scribes write that thoughout the 1890s the Kings County Council struggled
with the question of amalgamating their poor houses into one; however, it was
not until 1921 that the councillors found a site for the new home in Waterville.[224]
In November 1922, inmates from the three old poor houses were transferred to
the Waterville Poor House. The old properties were then sold. The county had
purchased the 90-acre tract of land for $2500.[225]

The *Wolfville Acadian* newspaper of December 1922 reports:

> The amalgamation of the Poor Districts of Cornwallis, Horton and
> Aylesford in this county has now been effected and the new building for
> the accommodation of the unfortunate poor which has been under con-
> struction during the past summer is now completed and has been taken
> possession of by the officials who have charge of this responsible and
> important branch of the municipality's affairs...The new edifice is situ-
> ated on elevated ground and commands a fine view of the surrounding
> country. The main structure which faces the south is 36 x 37 feet with

a wing on the north-east and 36 x 48 feet. It includes a large basement, main floor and attic. The main floor has a large plaza on the south about 75 feet in length. Adjoining are the men's smoking-room, kitchen, dining room and recreation room on the east-end, with the apartments for the superintendents and officials in this wing at the same end. At the west-end are similar rooms for women for sewing, recreation and dining rooms. The men's and women's recreation-rooms are connected by folding-doors which may be opened when required for any special occasion. There are two fireplaces for the men and the same for the women. Some of the wards or rooms are also located on this floor.

On the second floor are the dormitories for both males and females, the latter using the western part. A long hall running the entire length of the building divides by three doorways and provides as far as is possible for the plan for the segregation of the sexes.

The attic provides quarters for the help. There is also a promenade with fire-escapes located at either end. The basement is of concrete and is divided into furnace-rooms, work-shops, morgue, etc., with ample provision for fuel storage.[226]

The Waterville Poor House continued to operate until 1972. Shortly after it closed, the building was renovated and began operations as a shelter for children with severe mental challenges. In 1979, this facility was closed and later in that year, the building was demolished. The road on which this building stood, however, is still in existence and is called the County Home Road.

West Hants Poor House

West Hants County Poor Farm in Newport, on the Meander River. It opened in 1884 and closed in 1966. Photo courtesy of Dr. Allan E. Marble.

The West Hants Poor Farm in Newport opened its doors in 1884.[227] Dr. Page, inspecting the facility in 1888, described it as:

> Four stories high including basement and attic. The kitchen and dining room are in the basement. The inmates number forty-four, and unlike other similar institutions recently visited, a large proportion – twenty-three – aged eighteen months to eleven years.[228]

Like most of the asylums in Nova Scotia, this one admitted people with mental health issues, housing them together with poor people and children and providing no treatment for them. As it was the only tax-subsidized facility in that area besides the jail, it became the repository for people who did not fit the "norms" of their communities.

In 1892, Dr. Page wrote in his report that there were 42 inmates in the asylum; one had died and one or two had escaped. He commended the house for being "clean, comfortable and well managed."[229] In 1899, the new inspector, Dr. Sinclair, in addition to also noting that "the housekeeping is excellent," reported: "Children are here in large numbers." [230] There were 41 inmates living in the poor farm of which four were "insane." One of his final comments was about the cesspit: "Some plan should be devised to do away with the open slop-pool, which stands as a menace to health, almost in front of the house."

In 1977, a group of students from nearby Acadia University and Windsor High School wrote a book called *Gateway to the Valley*, which was published by the Town of Windsor. In it they wrote about the poor farm, which was called the County Home by then:

> A county Home was built at Newport to house those people who were (Poor and insane) "disorderly, drunkards, stubborn children or servants, beggars, fortune tellers," * lewd people or people who would not support their families. The Home became a dumping ground for the destitute or insane in the area, who were confined there by law and made to work, their board at the time being paid by the Town.[231]

By 1922, the home was called the Hants West Industrial Home and by the 1930s, the inmates were called patients. By 1952, the superintendent of the facility described the conditions in the Home as deplorable and called upon the Hants West Warden to improve the conditions immediately. The superintendent demanded that if these problems were not solved, he would no longer continue working there. Reforms to the institution followed quickly.[232]

The facility was closed by 1966 and the property, with the exception of the portion of land that had served as a cemetery, was sold off.

Chapter 4

African Nova Scotians, the Mi'kmaq and Poor Relief

African Nova Scotians and Poor Relief

It is often believed that African-descended people first came to Nova Scotia in the early 1780s, brought by white Loyalists refugees as their "slaves." In addition, many Black Loyalists, who had been freed by the British and promised land in exchange for their help in the American Revolutionary War, arrived in the province then. However, there is evidence of enslaved Africans residing in Nova Scotia earlier than that time. T. Watson Smith points out: "Slaves were brought into Nova Scotia at an early period ... That any were brought to ... Annapolis, or to Canseau ... is uncertain, as no records kept by the earliest Episcopal chaplain at the former place were to be found."[233]

The first recorded African to arrive in Nova Scotia was Mathieu de Costa. He was a translator who came to Annapolis Royal with Samuel de Champlain in 1605 to help build a relationship with the local Mi'kmaq. He was a free black man who spoke French, Dutch and Portuguese.[234] The African-descended people who followed after DeCosta were not in such an enviable position.

The presence of enslaved Africans is found in the records of Halifax shortly after it was settled in 1749, in the form of letters, inventories, wills and newspaper advertisements searching for "runaway servants" who are described as "negro."[235] Indeed, many of the streets that still exist in the City of Halifax and other townships and villages in the province are named after former slave owners.

One of the earliest registry books in the town of Bridgetown, Annapolis

County, records the sale of a "Mulotta" girl named Louisa, in July 1767, to a family in Annapolis Royal. The census of January 1, 1771, records "seven Negroes" in the township of Annapolis Royal.[236] The "servant for life" or "slave," as they were termed in legal documentation of that time, were often brought to Nova Scotia by their white "master." Some came to Nova Scotia directly from England with their white "masters," while others were brought to the province from the eastern seaboard of the United States, where Newport, Rhode Island, was the northern centre of the African human slave trade.[237]

The African would have, at that time, lived with and served their masters and his family. Consequently, they would have been fed, clothed and sheltered, in conditions which may have been either comfortable or horrendous. Regardless, the African-descended person had no choice over their position in life at this time in our history.

The arrival of the white Loyalist refugees in the early 1780s from the American War of Independence also meant the arrival of many of their African slaves. As Nova Scotia still practised slavery, some of these Africans were still bound to their slave-owning families.[238]

Other former African slaves, however, were now free men and women, as they had been promised their freedom if they fought for Britain during the war. More than 2000 free Black Loyalists were brought to Nova Scotia in British ships and landed at Shelburne and Annapolis Royal. Many went on to form their own settlements at Birchtown (Shelburne County), Granville and Delaps Cove (Annapolis County; the foundations of this community are still visible but it is not well recorded historically, having been so remote), Jordanville, (then called Brindley Town, Digby County), Tracadie Road (Guysborough County) and Preston (Halifax County) among others. Birchtown was, at one time, known as the largest settlement of free black people outside of the continent of Africa.

In 1796, Nova Scotia saw the arrival of 500 Maroons from Jamaica, thus marking the second mass migration of free blacks into Nova Scotia. Many of the Maroons left the province to either return to Jamaica or to relocate to Sierra Leone in Africa by the time the Black Refugees had begun to arrive after the War of 1812 between Canada and the United States.[239]

In Shelburne, after the arrival of the Loyalists, a combined poor house and house of correction was established. The Black Loyalists, in the meantime, had moved outside of Shelburne and established their own community of Birchtown in an attempt to avoid racism and abduction for resale into slavery.[240] In the

Former slave and Black Loyalist Rose Fortune. Artist unknown; image courtesy Annapolis Heritage Society.

hamlet of Port LaTour, 64 kilometres up the coast from Birchtown, the black community preferred to take care of their own poor people and, to that end, petitioned to be exempted from the poor tax.[241]

Although Britain and its colonies, such as Canada, did not officially make slavery illegal until 1834, the practice of slavery had been diminishing in these places over the decades due to a combination of factors, including the opposition of law courts to slavery in British North America. In 1796, Lieutenant Governor Wentworth wrote to the Duke of Portland noting slavery had almost been "exterminated" in Nova Scotia.[242]

While slavery may have been "almost exterminated," there were still "Proprietors of Negroes" in Nova Scotia in 1808, with 28 of those proprietors being in Annapolis County, claiming ownership of "82 negro servants." A petition was started in the Town of Digby and presented in the House of Assembly in December, 1808 requesting, essentially, that the owners of the black servants be given recompense for having to give up their slaves and the labour that they performed. The Legislature agreed to defer it to another time for debate but never actually got to back to it.[243]

Many of the African-Nova Scotians were accustomed to farming due to their enforced labour on plantations in the southern United States. Most of the freed black people settled in communities around the province and eked out a living by farming, selling items they made, or hiring themselves out as labourers. However, the African-descended people suffered illnesses, death of the main money earner of the house and tragedies such as house fires. Racism would have also contributed several barriers to the ability of African-Canadians to support themselves and their families in Nova Scotia. Dr. Marble notes:

> By far the largest group of paupers in Nova Scotia, during pre-Confederation nineteenth century, were the Blacks ... Whereas the Blacks

represented about 3 percent of the population of Nova Scotia, they amounted to 4.5 percent of the inmates in the Poor House during that period ... Between 1802 and 1811 a total of 68 Blacks were admitted to the Halifax Poor House.[244]

In September 1814, nearly 700 African-descended refugees arrived in Halifax from the Chesapeake Bay area of Virginia, having availed themselves of the presence of the Royal Navy in Chesapeake Bay. This was a result of a proclamation issued by Vice Admiral Sir Alexander Cochrane on April 7, 1814, which stated that all black residents of the United States who came aboard any of the His Majesty's Ships would be transported to a British colony in North America. (Black Refugees were the former slaves who came to Nova Scotia via the Underground Railroad. Much of our history has the Underground Railroad ending in Ontario but many Black Refugees came to Nova Scotia by ships, fishing boats, etc. They came to Canada whenever they could get here – anywhere from the early 1700s to the 1860s, when slavery ended in the USA.) Of the 684 Black Refugees who arrived from Chesapeake Bay, 158 would be admitted into the Poor House. They were referred to as the Chesapeake Blacks. Dr. William B. Almon, the poor house surgeon, noted that a number of the refugees arrived "ill with dangerous and loathsome disorder ... chiefly dysentery and smallpox." Unfortunately, by March 1815, seventy four of the Chesapeake Blacks had died in the poor house of smallpox. By 1817, there were between three and four thousand African-descended people in the province.[245]

The government of Nova Scotia established a number of programs to assist the African-Nova Scotians in supporting themselves. A number were relocated to other settlements, such as Preston outside of Halifax, prior to the winter of 1816-17. Although the soil was rocky and not suited for farming, the new black settlers were expected to begin farming immediately and start to support themselves. Their crops of 1816 failed, as did most farmers' crops that year. It became known as "the year without summer," and was explained in later years as the result of Mount Tambora in Indonesia erupting in

DIGBY, 21ſt Jᴜɴᴇ 179².

RUN AWAY, Jofeph Odel and Peter Lawrence (Negroes) from their Maſters, and left Digby laſt evening, the firſt mentioned is about Twenty four years of Age, five Feet fix Inches high, had on a light brown Coat, red Waiſtcoat and thickfet Breeches, but took other Cloaths with him, he is a likely young Fellow with remarkable white Teeth.— The other is about five Feet eight Inches high, very Black had on lighteſh coloured Clothes.—Whoever will fecure faid Negroes fo that their Maſters may have them again. ſhall receive TEN DOLLARS Reward, and all reafonable Charges paid.

DANIEL ODEL,
PHILLIP EARL.

From the Halifax Gazette newspaper,
July 10, 1792.

April 1815.[246] The skies filled with volcanic dust, which the sun could not filter through, causing major crop failures all over the globe for three years. Despite the crop failure all over the province (and, indeed, the world), Lieutenant Governor Dalhousie, in a letter to Lord Bathurst, blamed the former "slaves" for the failure of their crops and questioned their ability to ever be able to support themselves:

> Permit me to state plainly to Your Lordship that little hope can be entertained of settling these people so as to provide for their families and wants – they must be supported for many years – Slaves by habit and education, no longer working under the dread of the lash, their idea of reform is idleness and they are therefore quite incapable of Industry.[247]

Dalhousie also made the suggestion that perhaps the Black Refugees should be returned to their masters in the United States, if their masters would forgive them for leaving, or else they should be sent to Sierra Leone in Africa. Dalhousie was taken seriously in his suggestions, for the Provincial Council recommended on April 30, 1817, that all rations would cease on the first of June and that all the Black Refugees who wished to return to the United States (as a slave, because the abolition of slavery in the U.S A. was still several decades away) would be provided with a means of getting there. Rations continued to be distributed, however, to the Black Refugees who were still farming on the "waste lands allotted" to them until Dalhousie put his foot down in October 1818. Rations to the Black Refugees were then ceased on the instructions of the Earl of Bathurst.[248]

Without the rations, the Black Refugees were reduced to starvation levels of despair and desperation. This led to an increase in crime and begging as the refugees struggled to survive. The numbers of African-Nova Scotians incarcerated in the prisons jumped tremendously at this point and most of the rest were living in "deplorable conditions," nearly freezing and starving. The provincial government realized that, if they were to stop this trend, they needed to give relief to the Black Refugees. The council voted money for the purchase of potatoes and grain to alleviate their hunger and strongly encouraged them to emigrate to other countries. Many of them were against moving anywhere to the south as they feared being forced into slavery once more. However, 95 Black Refugees did take up the offer and sailed to Trinidad in January 1821.[249]

Attempts were made again in 1836 to have the people of the black settlements of Hammonds Plains and Preston migrate to warmer climates. Not one single person took up the offer for fear of bondage, as the West Indies were rife with white slave owners and it would be a dangerous place for free black people.[250] They would rather live in a cold climate in Nova Scotia, and "they could neither be induced by persuasion, nor prevailed upon by argument, to quit their present misery," wrote Reverend Robert Willis to the House of Assembly.[251] Despite facing overt racism from both their neighbours and their government, along with periodic starvation and a cold climate that could kill them, the free Black Loyalists of the Southern United States felt safer in Nova Scotia and in other parts of Canada than they did in the countries and islands to the south.

As the African-descended refugees would not move from their settlements, the Legislature began to vote relief money for them in the 1840s. Monies were raised to build schools and churches, to provide seeds for the farmers and to help alleviate suffering. In 1858, however, the Legislature again terminated all assistance to the black communities. Between 1859 and 1867, there is no mention of financial assistance to the African-Nova Scotians in the annual Journals of Assembly. This, of course, caused a great deal of poverty and hardship amongst them and, as had been the case in 1818, these communities suffered from starvation and mortality.[252]

After the County Incorporation Act of 1879, however, poor houses were built to house the poor, the sick and the "insane" in every county but

African Nova Scotian men who were inmates of the Halifax County Poor Farm in Cole Harbour. Photo courtesy of Cole Harbour Farm Museum.

Guysborough, and African-Nova Scotians could apply to be admitted to their local poor house. The Report on Public Charities of 1881 for the Halifax Poor House notes the name and settlement that each of their inmates came from. For African-Nova Scotian inmates, the word "colored" in parenthesis was written in the columns. Some of the black inmates were from Nova Scotia, while others were noted as being from West Africa.[253]

In Bridgetown, approximately 25 kilometres down the road from Annapolis Royal, where so many Black Loyalists landed in the 1780s, the overseers of the poor built a new poor house for the local white paupers and established the old poor house just for "the coloreds." Dr. Sinclair writes in his annual Report on Charities in 1899:

> The colored paupers are cared for in a separate building, in the rear of the present one, of which, I judge, it was the predecessor. Mr. Lowe experiences much anxiety of mind for fear of fire occurring here. It is of wood, heated by stoves, and the habits of its occupants render the fear natural.[254]

Steven Laffoley writes in his book, *The Halifax Poor House Fire*, that black people were admitted as inmates to the poor house. His examination of the inquiry into the poor house fire of 1882 notes that the administrators, overseers and lawyers all tried desperately to blame the start of the fire on a black inmate who operated the boiler in the basement of the home.[255]

A photo of some of the male inmates of the Halifax County Poor Farm located in the Cole Harbour poor house shows that some of them are clearly African-Nova Scotians. Probably the only person in the photo who is not an inmate is the man standing in the back with a hat on his head and sporting a suit, tie and handkerchief. The photo is, unfortunately, undated.

The closure of the county poor houses and the advent of social assistance in 1958 meant that many families of all ethnicities, colours and persuasions could receive assistance while living with their families in their own homes. It did not mean, however, that life was suddenly good for poor people or, most particularly, non-white poor people. The systemic racism that still exists in our culture means that many descendants of these Black Refugees and Black Loyalists continue to be subjected to different conditions than white people in terms of jobs, housing, education and more.

The Mi'kmaq and Poor Relief

The African-Nova Scotians were not the only group of people who were actively discriminated against. The Mi'kmaq were also moved around the province with the attempt to keep the racism-induced wretchedness of the indigenous people out of sight of white, euro-centric communities. The Mi'kmaq suffered a great deal from poverty, illness and starvation, and they died horrible deaths because of the historic (and continuing) racism that exists in this province. As is the case with African-Nova Scotians, the Mi'kmaq suffered under the government to an extent that cannot, with space limitations, be accurately recorded here. It has been proven a difficult task to find the voices and experiences of poor people in poor houses around the province; it has been even more difficult to find and record the voices of the African-Nova Scotians and even moreso of the Mi'kmaq.

It is known that the Mi'kmaq population was decimated by disease, poverty and warfare with the British within years of the arrival of Cornwallis and the succeeding British governors. Although the Mi'kmaq fought back, sometimes at the instigation of the French, the British almost eliminated the indigenous people and drove out most of the French population, particularly through what is now known as the Expulsion of the Acadians, from 1755 to 1764. In addition, the imposition of a foreign culture and religion upon the Mi'kmaq almost vanquished the First Nation as a people.

Reverend D. Luther Roth wrote in 1890 regarding the Mi'kmaq: "Whatever the Roman Catholic religion may have done to benefit his soul it has standing against it a heavy debt account, in what the vices of civilization and the impositions of the white man have done to the injury of his body."[256]

Even Lieutenant Governor Wentworth was moved by the poverty of the Mi'kmaq and wrote to the British colonial secretary in London in January 1802, expressing "a desire if possible to reclaim these wretched people, whose situation is deplorable, and sufferings extreme." Silence from London was the response.[257] In 1813, the newly arrived Walter Bromley appealed to the citizens of Halifax and the government of Nova Scotia with a project to make that year the one which saw "the emancipation [of the Mi'kmaq] from a state worse than slavery." Over the next several years, Bromley was successful in raising funds to transform the Mi'kmaq at Shubenacadie into farmers and the project appeared to be successful. In 1819, however, the Roman Catholic Church became concerned about the extent of Bromley's influence over the Mi'kmaq. Bromley was an Anglican. Allan Marble writes: "Thus the clash of the two religious doctrines terminated a plan which had the potential of demonstrating that the Mi'kmaq could, once more, function independently of the white man."[258]

That the Mi'kmaq were in poor houses has been recorded in the List of Paupers in the Poor House at Halifax. The years 1802 to 1811 show that there were 14 Mi'kmaq inmates.[259] However, the racist British colonial policies had such a terrible impact on the Mi'kmaq that most of them were suffering in poverty and starvation throughout the province. Dr. Marble writes that only 50 years after the arrival of the British in Halifax, the Mi'kmaq were in a terrible position. "By 1799 the Mi'kmaq in the vicinity of Halifax were described as paupers and were said to be entirely dependent on the inhabitants of Halifax for their maintenance during the winter."[260] Much of this poverty was due to the influx of thousands of Loyalist refugees and European immigrants who displaced the Mi'kmaq from their traditional hunting and fishing grounds and subsequently from the reserves of land set aside for the Mi'kmaq to survive upon.[261]

Dr. Gesner, a farmer, medical doctor and inventor of kerosene, which started the hydrocarbon industry, was for a time the commissioner for Indian Affairs. His report of December 21, 1857, was of a depressed nature: "On most of the reserves, begging was a common occupation ... they were a discouraged and spirit broken people."[262] He claimed, however, as so many white people did at that time and continue to do so today, to not understand the barriers of racism and poverty: "The gifts made to them from time to time have increased their indulgence in idleness and vagrancy."

It is questionable whether a historically nomadic people could or would want to become farmers, staying in one place on the land, when their traditions of thousands of years spoke to them of hunting, gathering and moving about with the seasons. Apparently, this did not cross the minds of the policymakers, nor did it occur to them that they should give a grant of proper lands and equipment to the Mi'kmaq while attempting to assimilate them. In a situation similar to what was done to the African-Nova Scotians, land and farming utensils were provided to the Mi'kmaq. However, the annual reports of the commissioners of Indian Affairs in the years 1842 to 1867 indicate that the soil they were given to farm upon was poor and rocky, the farm implements and seed supplied were insufficient and no one actually taught the nomadic people how to farm.[263] The Mi'kmaq were set up to fail and the failure was put upon their shoulders rather than the shoulders of the policymakers for their lack of insight.

Over time and struggle, the Mi'kmaq were relocated onto lands referred to as reserves. Mi'kmaq scholar Daniel N. Paul writes:

By 1821 the acreage set aside for the Mi'kmaq in the entire colony had reached a "princely" total of 20,765 acres. This great estate of swamps, bogs, clay pits, mountains and rock piles represented a tiny fraction of one percent of Nova Scotia's land base. The arable land in the entire grant was probably less than 200 acres.[264]

Although the Mi'kmaq could apply to be sheltered in a poor house, many were instead shuttled to these reserves of poor land, forced into "Indian schools" on the reserves and severely punished for speaking their language or practising their culture. The British colonizers tried very hard to assimilate the Mi'kmaq.

Although it is rare to see reference to the Mi'kmaq in the annual reports on the poor houses, the 1890 report contains a very sad story about a young Mi'kmaq girl. Dr. Page writes in his report on the Shelburne Poor House from his visit in 1889:

When I visited this house last year I found a little Indian girl with threatened disease of the spine and suggested that she be sent to the Victoria General Hospital, where I thought it quite probable the disease could be arrested by appropriate treatment, and her health restored. I consulted the hospital authorities and found them willing and ready to receive and treat her. I immediately wrote to the keeper, urging him to try and have her sent on. He handed my letter to some official, but before action was taken the Indian relatives came and claimed her under the impression, I understood, that they would get paid for the care of her. The result was that only a few days before my recent visit, she was brought back, suffering greatly, and in a most hopeless condition, with two open abscesses communicating with the spine, and very much emaciated, with no prospect but suffering or death. She is now being treated with every care and kindness, but it is too late.[265] [The next year, Dr. Page writes:] There were four deaths during the year, including the little Indian girl mentioned last year.

It is with a lack of understanding of poverty that Dr. Page wrote his cruel comments about the young girl's family. It is entirely reasonable to suppose that when the girl became sick, her family did what they could to help her heal even though they were mired in the deep poverty that was imposed on them by colonization. When they couldn't help her, they did the next best thing and took her to the poor house to be taken care of there. However, when the family found out that they might get some money and medicine (traditional or white medicine) to help them with her care and be able to keep their young daughter with them, they may have jumped at the opportunity. Once they had her back and found out there was no financial aid forthcoming and she was getting worse, they again did what they could to help her out by returning her to the poor house for comfort, food and care. They returned to their poverty to mourn the impending death of one of their daughters. It is so easy to employ racism and classism in placing blame on people in poverty without looking at all the extenuating circumstances.

Although the settlement of white Europeans In Nova Scotia almost brought the Mi'kmaq to extinction, they prevailed and have been bringing their culture and history back to the descendants of the grandparents who suffered so greatly. This is not to say that racism toward the Mi'kmaq does not still exist and is not systemic. The Mi'kmaq still struggle to gain decent paying jobs and an education that includes their history and experiences, and they still struggle against the barriers that are thrown up against them.

Chapter 5

The Elderly and People with Disabilities

The Poor of Digby Enquiry of 1885 did not just examine the tragic case of Charlotte Hill. It also tells the story, through bits and pieces of testimony from witnesses, of Louisa Jane Lewis. We first meet up with Louisa on page 1a of the commissioner's report, where she is described as "a confirmed lunatic," and they also write that "she is dangerous, and her language and conduct such as to make her an unfit inmate for a respectable house." The report goes on to say:

> An effort was made this spring to have her placed in the Insane Asylum, but the application was refused on the ground that she was incurable … She has several times managed to escape from her keepers and run at large for a few days before she could be hunted up and brought back, and as a result of these escapades she has increased the paupers of the county by several illegitimate children.[266]

(Note the language, which describes her not only as an animal but also puts the responsibility for having children out of wedlock squarely on her shoulders. Basic biology says she did not get pregnant by herself.)

On page 23 of the enquiry report, the pauper Eddie Burton Lewis gives testimony to Messrs. J.J. Ritchie and J.A. Smith and was also cross-examined by Messrs. T.C. Shreve, Q.C., and R.G. Munroe:

> While at Thomas' a girl named Louisa Jane Lewis had a child; she was partially insane; she had to work before confinement sometimes; have

seen Thomas beat her; have seen him box her ears three times and tie her hands with a rope; I thought the blows pretty rough; it was because she could not peel apple properly; her hands were tied with rope before her on bare wrist; this was about two months before her confinement.

On the same page of the enquiry report, we read testimony from Louisa's father, Morgan Lewis:

She was received aid as a pauper for some time; remember her at Watson Haight's, back of South Range; went to see her there; she said something a little out of the way to him and Haight struck her in the face with his fist and knocked her against partition; hard blow.

Upon cross examination by Shreve, Lewis said that Haight was a second cousin of his and that he had nothing to do with placing his daughter there. He had heard that his daughter was sent there and he did not object. Lewis further testified:

[The] girl was violent at times; used to tear her clothing; she is not so insane now as she was some years ago; lived with me till she went on the town; violent with me; won't swear she was at Comeau's a couple of years before she was a Haight's; she was chained in a pen to the side of the house; there were cracks in the side of the house; I could not have lived there 24 hours.

We don't meet up with Louisa Jane Lewis again until page 35 of the enquiry report, when Johnson Thomas, a poor master in Barton, District 2, is testifying. He tells of having boarded Louisa as well:

Have had Louisa Jane several times; first in 1880, immediately after Joe Nick Tibo was arrested ... supplied her with food and clothing; had trouble with her; had to tie her or shut her up, but not both at the same time; I had to tie her because she would run away, get into trouble, become pregnant and make great trouble; had to shut her up because her language and actions were most violent and outrageous; tied her hands in front of her with a handkerchief; had to tie her sometimes once a month, sometimes twice a week; could not have lived with her in the house unless; she would have killed some of us; she would strike us; after we had tied her she would promise to behave herself and we would untie her; ran away once to Yarmouth and again the same year to Truro; they sent her back both times.

The last we see of Louisa Jane is on page 39 of the report, where Mary Thomas, wife of Johnson Thomas, testifies about the poor in Digby. She states that she and her husband keep the poor and had seven poor at their house at that moment:

Louisa Jane Lewis is stopping with us since New Year's Day; she has a fearful disposition when mad; swears and blackguards and handles her child roughly; may become this way every day and again not for a fortnight; have treated her the same as my own family; same to eat as we, ourselves; I provide her with clothing as comfortable as that of my own family; she never complained.

Mary Thomas goes on to say that Louisa Jane has never been punished by her because she is "much too afraid of her for that." However, Mary Thomas then explains how Louisa Jane has had her hands tied with a handkerchief at her house, but she did not remember for what reason or when it happened. Mary Thomas also explains that her husband "boxed" Louisa Jane's ears as she was peeling the apples and spoiling them. "After my husband slapped her she behaved pretty well."[267] There is no further information on what happened to Louisa Jane, whose only crime was being mentally ill, or just rebellious.

As a poor house inmate you are expected to "earn your keep," but what happens when you cannot because you have a physical or mental disability? Even small children in the poor house were expected to do some form of work once they were old enough to walk and understand instructions. But residents who could not physically move, suffered from a mental illness and could not follow instructions, or were elderly and bedridden could not contribute to their life in a poor house. Those who were injured while employed would have very little to no recourse for financial compensation as workers' compensation rights legislation was not passed until 1914. The disabled worker would face financial ruin and end up in a local poor house. Author and historian Cheryl Desroches writes:

All state institutions relied on the work of inmates to be financially viable; however, and once again, those who were old and unable to work were increasingly marginalized and many were transferred to the cheapest form of institutional care — county poor farms.[268]

Prior to the establishment of asylums, poor houses and almshouses in Nova Scotia, paupers with mental illness would have been auctioned off alongside the healthy poor. People would have bid on the elderly and the "insane" as a means of getting whatever work they could out of them while also receiving an income for keeping them. The commissioners of The Poor of Digby Enquiry in 1885 interviewed several neighbours about the conditions under which the elderly were kept in the houses where they were "boarded." Mrs. Brennan, an elderly woman who had been boarded by many different families, was brought up several times during interviews, along with Joe Beaman and William Small, all of whom died while being boarded. Desroches writes: "The Halifax bridewell or workhouse ... housed a range of individuals in need of assistance, and in 1763, three rooms were set aside specifically for the poor who were unable to work."[269]

Many of the inmates of poor houses were people in these situations; elderly people who had either no family members willing to take care of them or no family members at all. People did not "retire" until well into the 20th century. Prior to that, family members would take care of their elderly. But agricultural society was becoming mechanized and farm life and family support were dissolving. Elderly persons without family were turning to poor houses to live out the end of their lives. Desroches points out:

> Increasingly, the aged within state funded institutions were funneled from provincial hospitals into the cheapest form of institutional care – municipal poor farms. Badly neglected, at the turn of the century, these run-down facilities became the earliest nursing homes for the aged in Nova Scotia.[270]

People who were considered "insane," which covered a broad spectrum of conditions and mental illnesses, were brought to the poor houses as an asylum for the family of the "insane" person. The family may not have been able to cope with the mental illness of the afflicted person, or the family members may have died, leaving this as the only option. As poor houses often doubled as hospitals, those with incurable diseases or conditions would end up there to be cared for as well as possible. Desroches writes:

> Townships, lacking the funds to provide for their indigent, increasingly sent them to Halifax creating an almost constant state of over-crowdedness in the Halifax Poor Asylum that housed an indiscriminate variety of individuals – the sick, the insane, and the old who had nowhere else to go.[271]

The annual Reports on Public Charities provide the numbers of "insane" at the poor houses and asylums. Most poor houses made very little effort to keep the paupers from the mentally ill, and one could argue that this is indicative of the prevalent attitude of the day toward the poor – that poverty was a mental illness and that mental illness and poverty were offensive. Poverty can also make a person mentally ill.

Some of the poor house staff tried to have the mentally ill participate in work that would engage them, work that they could do. Inspector Sinclair described the situation in the Arcadia poor house in his 1899 report:

> At my first inspection there were some very young children who were placed in charge of insane women, the matron saying it was impossible to get any other to care for them. A risky business, I should imagine.[272]

The nature of the "insanity" is generally not noted in the reports other than by the categorizations of "harmless insane," "violent insane," and "lunatic."

Institutions for the mentally ill were established in the Maritimes during the 1840s and 1850s, such as the Mount Hope Asylum outside of Dartmouth.[273] Persons who were considered "insane'" would be sent there for treatment by doctors from around the province. The asylums quickly became filled to capacity. When the poor houses were built, the "harmless insane" were kept at those facilities instead of being sent to the asylum outside of Dartmouth. However, the "insane" that were considered incurable would not be accepted into the asylums as, it is supposed, the asylums did not want to become a warehouse for "incurably insane" people, or "lunatics" in the language of the day.

The poor houses and poor farms might have been a better option for some patients with mental illness in that they had a chance of having a sympathetic poor house keeper – or perhaps not. Edward Robicheau, a man from the Weymouth area, was interviewed in 1985 about the Marshalltown Almshouse, outside of Digby. He told a reporter from the *Digby Courier* that he was born in 1935 but related stories that his great uncle told him about the treatment of the poor at the poor farm. He claimed he had verified his uncle's stories with other people. It is interesting that he spoke of the plight of mentally ill people, in particular mentally ill women who were pregnant:

> If a young lady was taken there and had a long list of mentally ill in her family, she was made to do extra duties hoping she would have a miscarriage. After she had the baby, nothing was done to keep the babies alive and they were generally thrown in the furnace.[274]

Was this story true? It is difficult to say. The events that Mr. Robicheau spoke of would have happened around the same decade as the Chester Ideal Maternity Home was in operation. In that institution, infants who were less than "ideal" – physically disabled, of mixed race, not Caucasian, or showed early signs of conditions such as Downs Syndrome – were intentionally neglected and left to die. This chilling tragedy was well documented in the book *Butterbox Babies* by journalist Bette Cahill.[275]

Mental illness and conditions associated with ageing were beginning to receive specifically targeted medical care. These new ideas were demonstrated in the design of the new, and last, Halifax Poor House, built in 1869 on the corner of Inglis and Robie Streets. As discussed previously, believing that the aged and mentally ill would benefit from the fresh air on the top floor of the new institution, the architects designed a hospital ward on the third floor of the three storey building. However, the elevator only went to the second floor, not to the floor where the sick, the mentally ill and the aged were housed. On the night of November 6, 1882, a fire broke out in the basement and most of the victims of the tragic fire, which destroyed the Halifax Poor House, were bedridden on the third floor and could not get out of the building.[276]

As the "modern" social services policies were developed, the elderly were the first group of people to be considered. History professor and author Suzanne Morton writes: "The economic vulnerability of the elderly and their sometimes dependent state meant that the aged, along with widowed mothers and orphans, were at the forefront of the development of the welfare state."[277]

The federal Old Age Pension was put into place in 1927; however, Nova Scotia did not participate until 1934. Eventually, many of the poor houses in Nova Scotia were transitioned into seniors' homes or residential centres for those with severe mental illnesses or disabilities. Many of these institutions were built on the grounds of former poor houses.

Chapter 6

Death in the Poor House

> Here I lie by the chancel door;
> They put me here because I was poor.
> The further in, the more you pay,
> But here I lie as snug as they.[285]

In the *Digby Courier* newspaper of March 6, 1985, Edward Robicheau spoke in an interview about what his great uncle had told him about life in the Marshalltown Almshouse, outside of Digby. His great uncle had related what happened after an inmate died:

> In the case of death, many were buried on the place. They had grave-yards there. The inmates staying here looked after the dead and built their own coffins in the basement. They would put a person in a rough box right off the bed, take him down in the field and bury him just like an animal. There was a man from the North Range area who had died at the Poor Farm. He went to the Catholic Church in Plympton to be buried. The Priest had to review the remains – that was part of his job. When he opened the rough box, the man in question was in the rough box without a stitch of clothes on, just lying on an old blanket that wasn't fit to take to the dump.[279]

Mr. Robicheau's great uncle described a funeral scenario that was common for more than a century when dealing with the death of an inmate of a poor

106

house in Nova Scotia (and probably neighbouring provinces). Many of the poor houses around Nova Scotia have unmarked cemeteries for the poor who were buried there.

Scholar Cynthia Simpson also explores this subject:

> Interestingly, though inmates were employed to manufacture coffins for the town and local hospitals, they were also fabricating their own final resting place ... The inmates of the Saint John County almshouse in New Brunswick "performed the grim tasks at the Dead House – making coffins, shrouds and interring unclaimed bodies of almshouse inmates and others." Though no record of the Halifax poor house inmates interring the dead was found, one may linger on the assumption that their duties were similar to those of neighbouring provinces.[280]

Edward Robicheau's re-telling of his great uncle's descriptions of life in the Marshalltown poor house confirms this assumption. When an inmate died in a poor house, if no one from their family stepped forward to claim the body and bury them, the poor house would take responsibility and bury them in a plain pine box in an unmarked grave. There was no money for marking the passing of a pauper. Simpson writes:

> The burial location of the poor served only to reaffirm the subordinate lot they held in life as they were most often relegated to a potter's field, public squares, or sections of the cemetery unwanted by those of higher status.[281]

In an article written for *The Coast*, a Halifax newspaper, on October 29, 2015, Maura Donovan writes:

> While the new Central Library is a hive of activity, the disused hulk of its predecessor sits down the street quiet as a grave. Fitting, as there's an actual graveyard underneath the old library property on Spring Garden Road. This may come as a surprise to some, since there's no interpretative panel, plaque or marker to give away what lies beneath ... and there never has been.[282]

The remains of thousands of paupers lie under what was, at one time, a courthouse for the city of Halifax, and later became the city library. Dr. Allan Marble estimates that the number of individuals buried in this poor house burial ground is close to 4500 – 2480 officially recorded paupers' deaths and 1700 unrecorded paupers' deaths.[283]

Paupers in a poor house died without the full mourning customs that were extended and paid for by the wealthier class. There was no laying out of the body, no shroud, no funeral procession, no burial ceremonies, no private burial ground and certainly no headstone to mark their graves and acknowledge their lives. Often, burial of paupers took place during the night. It was the end of a life, a hasty burial in a cheap pine box with only the grave digger to witness the pauper's interment to the earth. Sadly, "the poor person's funeral came to be viewed as 'the final stamp of failure.'"[284]

Once a poor person got to the grave, however, that did not mean that they finally got the rest and peace they believed they would once they died. According to Simpson, when a poor house pauper died, the family had six weeks to claim the body of their deceased family member. Otherwise, the poor house had the option of recouping the cost of supporting the pauper by selling the cadaver to a medical school. As Simpson writes, sometimes the family of the poor did not claim the body – not because the financial burden of the death was too great but because the negative stigma attached to having a family member in the poor house and the shame it brought upon them was too great.[285]

The Honorable Judge Fetch in Halifax kept diaries and letters from the period 1776 to 1835. In a December 1801 letter to a friend in Boston, he writes:

> Doctor ....burst into my study with what he called "joyful news" ... his news was of a recent appointment as surgeon to the Poor House. You laugh but the "Systems Monger" thinks this is a great achievement. I believe I know why. He can now experiment to his heart's content on those who have neither the intelligence nor the freedom to make objection to his poking, prodding, lancing and leeching ... I expect he and his like will soon make the Poor House into a Surgeon's Hall with a constant batch of live and not so live specimens.[286]

The judge's letter suggests that the poor were used for medical experiments in their illness and in their death. The medical society considered the bodies

Arcadia Poor Farm Cemetery, at the end of the Yarmouth Airport Runway. The cemetery is on government land surrounded by high fences with No Trespassing signs all around. The cemetery is marked by a run-down fence and rotting wood cross. Photo by author, May 2017.

of "the diseased poor" as suitable subjects for young surgeons to learn about anatomy and diseases, and, they justified to themselves, allowed the poor to pay back their debt to society for being inmates in a poor house. When families did show up to collect the body of their loved one, they could have been refused the right to claim their family member's body. The authorities believed that families forfeited their right to the body of their poor house family member because they did not take care of them in life, and therefore they should not be permitted to take care of them in death.[287]

If a family did not claim their family member's body after six weeks (during which time a body could become quite rank in decomposition) and the body was not offered up to the medical school as collateral for their time in the poor house, they would be buried in an unmarked grave in the land around the poor house. In the case of the Halifax Poor House, the graves were dug so shallow, in an attempt to save money, that the people of Halifax complained about the smell. T.B. Atkins writes of this in his book *History of Halifax City*:

The rock wall that surrounds the former Middlefield Poor House in Queens County. The dead of the poor house are recorded as being buried along the rock wall. Photo by author July 2017.

The Poor House Burial Ground, at the corner opposite the present new Courthouse, was at this time a standing nuisance in consequence of the want of drainage and the careless manner in which the bodies of paupers were interred.[288]

Another historian, Thomas Raddall writes:

There must have been many an edifying spectacle for the gentlefolk sniffing the flowers across the way. There poor house dead were buried hastily in shallow graves in the yard, and for many years there were complaints about the smell which hung over this part of Spring Garden Road.[289]

In a crowded poor house, several deaths might take place at the same time, especially during an epidemic such as smallpox. As a result, to save money, several coffins were placed in the same grave at the same time. "Communal pauper funerals were a common occurrence in the workhouse where 'one service catered for all pauper burials taking place that day.'"[290] Although there is no evidence that this happened at the Halifax Poor House, it may be assumed that if the need arose, this would have taken place.

Then there was the concern about grave robbers. If a pauper's body made it into a shallow grave in the poor house cemetery, there were threats of having their dead bodies dug up by grave robbers who would sell their bodies to medical schools or doctors for dissection. Simpson writes:

> Rampant overseas and in America in the nineteenth century, dead paupers and lunatics were favoured by body snatchers, who roamed burial grounds, digging up corpses and selling them to anatomists for 2 to 14 guineas.[291]

Judge Fetch writes in his diary on March 28, 1792:

> Since the discovery in the Poor House Burying Ground of two graves opened and robbed of the corpses, the town's medical men shun the public market and the busy haunts where they customarily sup and take a glass. My own club meetings vibrate with ridicule.[292]

Today, many of the communities which had a poor house and an attached unmarked cemetery have organized a committee to raise funds to clear the overgrown graveyard and to mark the graves that they can find or at least erect a cairn or a plaque to honour the dead buried here. Groups in Greenwich, Waterville, Cole Harbour, Bridgetown, Truro and many other communities have worked diligently to give respect to dead paupers in this manner. Halifax, on the other hand, has not acknowledged its dead paupers. In a twist of cruel irony, across Spring Garden Road from the paupers' unmarked graves lies the Old Burying Ground, a place of pride for the city of Halifax. This beautiful and historic grave-

Arcadia Poor Farm Cemetery. Photo by author, May 2017.

yard does contain the burial sites of nine Mi'kmaq and 29 African-Canadians, however, the majority of the people buried there are wealthy people with fine stones, markers and mausoleums to mark their burial places. Even in our present time, this fine cemetery receives federal taxpayers' monies to restore and maintain the burial place of the comfortably rich, while the poor across the street remain unmarked, unacknowledged and forgotten simply because they did not have any money[293].

Chapter 7

---·◆·---

Whispers from the Poor House

In 1920, Lita Saulnier was just a young woman when she entered the poor house in Meteghan. She was ill. No one was quite certain what she was ill with, but Lita was admitted to the poor house nonetheless. She was thought to have contracted diphtheria, so the poor house administration put her alone in what was referred to as a 'strong room' in the basement. Strong rooms were used to keep 'inmates' of the poor house in a room they could not break out from. The inmates put in there could be violent, criminal or contagious with disease. Lita received her meals through an opening in the door to her room, passed out her soiled laundry, received fresh laundry and associated with none of the other poor house inmates.........for 40 years![294]

It was only after the poor house keeper retired and a new person was put in place in 1960 that Lita Saulnier was rediscovered. The new poor house keeper was appalled by Lita Saulnier's plight. Lita was brought out of the strong room cell, however by this time she had forgotten how to speak.[295] She spent the remainder of her years at a home for the aged in Yarmouth, regained some of her speaking abilities and passed away in the early 1980s.[296]

In *Poverty, Poor Houses and Private Philanthropy*, the Senior Scribes write:

> In a letter to F.R. MacKinnon, Medard Comeau of Meteghan Centre reported:

> One inmate, (name deleted), developed diphtheria as a young person in her early twenties. She spent 40 years in the Saint Mary's Home in

an isolation room upstairs because they believed her to be infectious. When Mr. and Mrs. Comeau took over as Superintendent in 1965 they persuaded the medical authorities to send (name deleted) to Halifax where she was tested and sent back with a clean bill of health. After all these years of isolation it was obvious that (name deleted) had lost all her capacity to function as a normal human being. She was transferred from Saint Mary's Poor House when it closed to Villa Acadienne. On September 8, 1975 she was transferred to Harborside Lodge in Yarmouth where she died in 1983.[297]

According to author Lance Woolaver, Lita Saulnier's case is not the only one such as this. He writes "A poor house in Halifax would contribute an account of a woman kept in an underground cage."[298] The horror of such abuse would be indescribable.

How did Lita Saulnier cope? How did she feel upon her release? We do not know as she never wrote down what happened and no one ever recorded her story.

The voices of those who spent time in a poor house have not been written down or recorded. Perhaps it was the stigma of being in a poor house. Perhaps an inmate did not want to record their feelings about being in a poor house for fear of appearing 'ungrateful'. The closest example of a first person account of an inmate in a poor house was written in a few letters to the editor of the Acadian Recorder more than a decade apart.

The first letter was published on October 30, 1819 and was written by a man calling himself Peregrinator. He writes of his washerwoman, Mrs. Soapsuds he calls her, who was:

"...soon overtaken with a serious distemper...she had been removed to the public Infirmary or what is a more appropriate name, the Poor House."

Peregrinator visited her in the Poor House and, upon being received by "...a most grotesque figure" was accosted for 'coppers for tobacco' for taking him to the washerwoman. The writer complied with a few coppers and was led to, first, the matron of the poor house and then to his washerwoman, who immediately burst into tears upon seeing him. Mrs. Soapsuds was ashamed to be '...in such a place as this', he writes.

Peregrinator writes that, upon looking around, he observed the place to be 'quite comfortable'. "Ah sir" Mrs. Soapsuds responds, "it is all show and a few of the miserable females you see here, however unable, are obliged to keep the place so clean as it is."

Mrs. Soapsuds then tells him that the doctor only comes once or twice a week as his private practice keeps him so busy, and that when he does come, he runs through the poor house with only a cursory visit with the inmates. Other young doctors come here as well, she tells him, but they seem to know 'little of the profession', suggesting that medicine students were learning from the illnesses and bodies of the poor house inmates.

The writer then asks her about the food that she receives, to which Mrs. Soapsuds replies: "...(we) receive but a little indian porridge and molasses three times a day – sometimes tea without milk and about a sufficiency of bread for a suckling infant." Peregrinator ends his lengthy letter to the editor with many suggestions for improving the poor house.[299]

Then, as now, some readers took offense to the idea that the poor may have ideas of their own about how they are treated and in calling for more humane considerations. Upon reading this letter, a writer calling himself Socius took offence with Peregrinator's letter and the washerwoman's observations. Socius writes that if we can judge a man by his companions, then we can have little respect for Peregrinator for keeping the companionship and visiting "...his diseased and garrulous washerwoman." Socius goes on to justify and challenge the diet that the washerwoman described, and questioned the intelligence of the washerwoman and Peregrinator, calling upon him to 'be silent'. Socius writes: "It is, therefore, at once base and ungrateful for any man to vent his spleen in gratuitous complaints, which may poison the minds of the indigent and the uniformed (sic)."[300]

Another letter to the editor of the *Acadian Recorder* a month later, written by Edward Hays, tells of his lack of medical treatment in the poor house and how he had to leave the poor house to be cured.

A letter to the editor in the *Acadian Recorder* newspaper was published on May 14, 1831. Using the pseudonym "A Grateful Hibernian," he wrote that he had become ill in the summer of 1830 and was not able to support himself when winter came. He applied for admittance to the Halifax Poor House and Asylum.

"Being a perfect stranger to the public institutions of Halifax, but more particularly to that of the Poor House, I must confess I was forcibly struck with the cleanliness, good order, and regularity, which prevailed

in the ward to which I was conducted and the cheerfulness and content-
ment which were visible in the appearance of its poor inmates."[301]

All these letters, however, describe what it was like or not like, in the hospital
portion of the poor house. Those who were residing in the poor house because of
a lack of income and money did not have their voices recorded. Some of the poor
house keepers, matrons and workers in the poor house, who could come and go
as they pleased, children of the poor house keepers, wrote or recorded what it was
like to live in the poor house. But the stories of the men, women and children
who lived there have been difficult, if not impossible, to find.[302]

Children were brought into the poor house with their parents and siblings;
often with just their mothers. Everett Lewis, husband of famed folk artist Maud
Lewis, went into the Marshalltown Almshouse (outside the town of Digby)
with his parents in 1901. His father was Edward Burton, mother Mary, sons
Haliburton, Boyd, Everett and Charles and daughters Lillie and Jessie. The
baby son, Charles, was adopted out of the poor house. They had previously
been on the family farm in Bear River before they moved to the Marshalltown
Almshouse.[303]

Ten years later, Everett's mother Mary got a job as a 'live-in domestic' in the
local area and had her 12 year old son Everett with her. The others remained in
the poor house, where several of them died – Everett's sister Lillie in 1920, his
father in 1936 and sister Jessie and brother Boyd in 1954.[304]

Bessie Lewis of Bear River must have had similar feelings about going to
the local poor house. In 1922, Bessie was a housemaid when she found herself
pregnant and not married. The shame of being an unwed mother was over-
whelming in such a small vil-
lage. Her only option would
be to go to the almshouse in
Marshalltown to have her
baby, where the child might
be adopted out if it survived
or she could stay there and
see her child raised in the
poor house. Either way, Bessie
Lewis would live with the
shame forever and would have

*Everett Lewis, painting by Steven Rhude. Photo by
Ernest Cadegan.*

difficulty ever finding a husband. Given this situation, Bessie decided to exercise the only other choice she felt she had; she threw herself into the water and died of 'suicide by drowning'.[306]

Senior Scribes write "As late as 1923, unwed expectant mothers who were not wanted at home were sent to the Almshouse to have their babies, and the newborn children were kept there as inmates."[307]

Quoting Edward Robicheau in a 1985 *Digby Courier* newspaper article: "Back in the earlier days, it was against the law for a young lady to come in a family way and not be married. She was taken there against her will and the child was taken out for adoption. After she spent her time there, she was free to go."[308]

Throughout research for this book, there are passing references made to 'widows' who were once 'great ladies' that are admitted to poor houses. The husbands may have died unexpectedly and with outstanding debts that must be paid; or if they abandoned the family, they left their wives and children penniless, without means of support. Women would not be hired for much more than nannies, teachers and housemaids and even then, they would not be paid enough to support their children let alone their previous lifestyles. In the style of Daniel Defoe's character in the book *Roxana*, the women must find a way to survive.[309] Many women, like the characters in Lance Woolaver's play *The Poor Farm*, were refugees from the sex trade.[310]

Author Steven Laffoley wrote of several stories of poor house inmates in his book *The Halifax Poor House Fire*.[311] It is fascinating to read of the life of inmates in the Halifax Poor House in 1882 and how they ended up there.

So what would have happened once an inmate entered a poor house? From the research for this book, generalizations can be made overall but from poor house to poor house there would be minor differences.

If you, the reader, became homeless, in poverty and decided that the poor house was the only place you could go to, how you would get there would depend upon the rules of your local poor house. You couldn't just show up at a poor house and expect to be taken in. Some poor houses wanted the pauper to have a recommendation of poverty from a person of status in the community, such as a minister or local politician. The pauper must also be known as a 'deserving' pauper. They must not have ended up in poverty because of alcohol, gambling or some other form of 'sin'.

At other poor houses, you could approach the front door and ask to speak with the poor house keeper or matron and request admittance. They would ascertain whether your need for accommodation at the poor house was required. If the poor house was overcrowded at the time, you would have to wait until they had room for you. This often meant you had to live on the street or in a barn or field until the poor house had room for you.

Once you entered the poor house, one of several things would happen: If you were with your children, they would be separated from you. If you were married, you would be separated from your spouse. There were no rooms for families or married couples – only dormitories separated by gender and for children. You were not permitted to speak to your other family members any more, depending upon which poor house you were admitted to. If you were single, you would be assigned to the dormitory of your identified gender.

Senior Scribes wrote: "Thus if an old couple had to end their days there, they were separated from each other. This was necessary because there were no bedrooms, just public dormitories and in some places, there might not have been even sheets."[312]

Once admitted to the poor house, you would be stripped of any possessions you had. This meant anything of value, including clothes. These would be sold to help pay for your stay or to help pay off any debts you owed when you entered the poor house.

Upon entrance, you would be stripped of your clothes. Laffoley writes:

Once inside the poor house, the new inmate's clothing would be removed and disinfected. This often involved heating in some fashion, leaving the garments literally the worse for wear...After being disinfected, the clothes were stored. The new inmate would be bathed and then inspected by the medical attendant to ensure no obvious infection was being brought into the house. At that point, the inmate was given a uniform to wear and was assigned a room in which to sleep.[313]

Inmates were given clothing to wear which was pretty much 'uniform' throughout Canada. "Men typically wore a knitted jacket, pants, a waistcoat and cloth caps...women wore a calf length plain dress...children wore variations of the same clothing."[314] Some poor house administration made the inmates wear a patch on their clothing indicating which parish or village they were from.[315]

Once you were assigned a bed, it did not necessarily mean that you had the bed to yourself. Bed sharing was common in poor houses even though the cots were made to sleep one person. In most beds, the mattresses were 'ticks' which even people who were not in poor houses slept on. A tick was a large sack made by sewing two sheets together and stuffing it with hay. Fresh hay would have smelled nice although it would not be good for anyone with allergies and would be lumpy. Hay that hadn't been changed in weeks or months could contain mould, bugs and dirt amongst other things. Coil mattresses would have come along later but might not have been changed for years at a time.

The sheets were changed, on average, once every two weeks. The sheets were often dirty rags, as were the blankets. Some poor houses did not provide sheets at all. The sick often slept together, as well as the healthy. Sometimes, when the poor house was overcrowded, an inmate might end up sleeping on the floor.

Your daily routine would consist of rising from bed sometime between 5am and 6am, depending upon the sunrise and the work the inmate was doing. You would make your way to the dining area for breakfast. Your breakfast would be plain and cheap, as a means of economizing and not making the poor house too comfortable for paupers. Your breakfast might consist of a cup of tea, bread and butter. Or it might consist of tea and a gruel made of oatmeal and flour.

You would then go to work to make money for your stay at the poor house. If you were a woman, you would spend your time either in the kitchen or the laundry. The kitchen would be preferable as it is warmer in the winter and food is accessible to you. In the laundry you would be washing by hand the clothing, sheets, blankets and any other items of the inmates and the poor house keeper and his family. You would also be sewing any repairs that were needed, cleaning the sleeping dormitories and all other rooms.

In some poor houses, the babies would be cared for by the matron of the poor house and other female inmates. Older children and elderly people would be sent to pick oakum from old tarry ropes used on ships and building sites. The oakum would then be pulled apart into fibres for recycling. It was hard work that often damaged the fingers of those doing it. In the Halifax Poor House, children and the elderly also made straw hats for women and men which were for sale to the public.

As times changed, some poor house children received some schooling either in the house or were sent to the local school. By the time they were adolescents, however, they were no longer considered children and were put to work.

If you were a man in a poor house, you would likely be sent to work out in the barn, in the fields (particularly if you were in a poor house, also called poor farms, in rural Nova Scotia), making stone fences or repairing them, tending to livestock, planting, hoeing, reaping garden produce, repairing buildings, cleaning outhouses, etc. In the Halifax Poor House, men were set to breaking stones for gravel for use on the roads in the city.

Laffoley writes of work in the Poor Houses of England:

A common job for men in the early Victorian poor house was bone crushing. The task involved using heavy metal ramrods to crush the bones of diseased inmates in order to create dust for fertilizer. In Andover, England, bone crushing created a minor scandal in 1845, when the practice became public knowledge. However, the outcry against the work was not a matter of offense taken by inmates crushing the bones of the poor house dead for fertilizer. *Rather the outcry arose when the public became aware that inmates were fighting over the scrap meat still found on the bones.* (emphasis mine)[316]

Work was paused for lunch at noon, which would consist of soup made of peas, vegetables, or cheap cuts of meat such as mutton. Bread would be served along with a small cup of beer for the men. Work would then resume from 1:00 pm until 6:00 pm, when supper would be served.

Supper would often consist of tea, bread, butter and cheese for the women. Men would get the same thing except they would get beer instead of tea. Children would get bread, butter and milk.

The after supper period was often left as a time of rest and recreation for the inmates. They could read, if literate, and if they could find a book, magazine or newspaper. They could talk amongst each other quietly but only with their own gender. Lights would be out at 8 pm, later in the summer seasons.

The weekends would consist of visitation by friends and relatives, if you had anyone to visit you. After church service on Sundays inmates generally met with visitors in a common area and had an hour with them. The inmates were generally allowed to rest on Sundays and, after supper, they would have speakers come in to give them lectures.

Laffoley quotes a poor house inmate in London, England:

Sunday is not a pleasant day in this house of ours...The Sabbath among us is a day of rest; emphatically so, or of stagnation rather. We have an hour longer in bed of a morning in the summer. We go to divine service once a day...and, immediately after supper, we have a troop of preachers let in upon us, who howl at us in the most uncompromising manner, without ever asking leave – very much against the will of many of us, indeed – from half-past six until bedtime."[317]

The days would continue, one after the other, until you managed to get out of the poor house; that is, IF you could get out. Some inmates had family who agreed to care for the inmate and take them out of the house; others were given jobs outside the poor house, some checked themselves out with the poor keeper's permission, many died trying to get out of the poor house. Others ran away.

In 1899, the Inspector Dr. Sinclair noted his concern about runaway inmates in his report on the Pictou County Poor House in Riverton. He wrote:

The privies are in detached cells, joined by covered passageways with the main building...it appears to me unsafe to have no protection or means to prevent a patient getting through the seat hole and falling or dropping into the cesspool fifteen or twenty feet below, at the imminent risk of broken bones or suffocation in liquid human manure...That no patient has, so far, attempted escape by this means is great good luck.[318]

One must wonder how bad the conditions must be in the poor house to consider the necessity of such an escape! Of course, there were good poor house keepers and matrons as well as bad. They had an enormous impact on how well an inmate would do, survive, get out or die in a poor house.

Although we do not hear from the actual voices of the poor in the poor houses, putting together testimony from articles, policies, research, second voices and reports tells us how inmates lived and how most were treated, both inside and outside the poor house. Either way, it was truly a horror for poor people.

Chapter 8

"Things are so much better now"

In the course of my research for this book, I have often heard people say statements like, "Thank heavens things are better now" or "Poverty was hard for people back in those days, not like today," and I know that this is a person who has not experienced poverty. They are speaking, of course, about the fact that people are no longer subjected to life in poor houses.

Some things for some people are better. In 1927, the Canadian government instigated the Old Age Pension and many elderly people no longer had to go to a poor house once they became too old to work and did not have any family to care for them. Add to that the Canada Pension Plan and the Guaranteed Income Supplement and things are somewhat better for senior citizens. The seniors who worked for low wages all their lives and the women who took time out from the workforce to raise children are still struggling, particularly if they are single seniors. However they can now be more autonomous in how they choose to live.

In 1958 the Elizabethan Poor Laws were formerly abolished in Nova Scotia. However the Settlement Policy, which was enacted in the time of King Henry VIII and brought to Nova Scotia with Cornwallis, was not removed from provincial legislative policy until the year 2000. The Canada Assistance Plan (CAP) was enacted in 1966 and, as its name suggests, assisted poor people who did not have jobs, could not qualify for Unemployment Insurance (as it was known then) and had no other source of income. The CAP was administered to assist those in need in their home provinces. In 1997, the CHST was enacted federally (Canadian Health and Social Transfer) and the CAP was removed. This was significant for people in poverty as the federal government now gave a lump sum to each of the provinces for health, education and social security, which the provincial government may distribute as it sees fit.[319] This was not good news for people on social assistance, as politicians recognize that distribution of anything to poor people is still not popular with most constituents.

As a result, Nova Scotia has seen a very low increase in social assistance rates since that time. Depending upon how much assistance a person receives, the increases have only been between .02% and .07% since 1997. There have been no increases in shelter rates. People on social assistance today are living on monies that were inadequate in 1996.

Much of our attitude toward poor people has not changed from the time of the Henry VIII. The belief that poor people are responsible for their own poverty is still prevalent. Our culture still believes that poor people made bad decisions somewhere along the line and that is why they are in poverty. So many people don't think beyond the superficial attitudes presented to them by church, government and their neighbours to examine the fact that policies from church and state have negatively impacted groups of people such as First Nations, African-Canadians, men, women, children and people not born into wealth. People in general blame poor people for their own state of poverty, calling them lazy, unmotivated, moochers and welfare bums. Even those who work for a living but are paid so poorly that they still must receive social assistance and help from a food bank are labelled with those names. On the other hand, wealthy people are given credit for being smart, without consideration of how they have grown their wealth, possibly by an inheritance or even an illegal activity. In Nova Scotia, for example, the illegal practice known as 'rum running' in the 1920s initiated the wealth of several families. Other families grew their wealth from unethical activities such as slave trading or slave owning, stealing money from the general public, insider trading on the stock market or other similar activities. Of course, some wealthy families did achieve their status through honest methods even though this can be very difficult to achieve. Some governments like to point fingers at poor people for the "cost" of social assistance when their budgets are overspent running a deficit. They do this to take attention away from the fact that they have overspent on other things, such as patronage positions and increases in their own pay and/or pensions.

Begging is illegal. In Henry VIII's day, beggars were branded on the ear and imprisoned. As I was writing this book, an "aggressive" beggar in the Halifax area (aggression is open to the interpretation of the accuser) was arrested and fined for begging. Despite the fact that the person is begging because he does not have any money, now he must pay a fine for begging on top of this? No offer for help. This is punishment for being poor.

The poor houses were mostly located outside of the towns. The first poor house/work house was located at what is now the bottom of Spring Garden Road and Barrington Street. In the 1750s, this location was outside the hub of activity of the new Town of Halifax, which was centred at the cove where the ferry terminal is now located. As Halifax grew, the poor house was moved further and further out from the centre. The poor houses that followed Confederation were, with exception of the Town of Pictou, outside of the towns. This may be partly because the poor house was also a poor farm and a location with arable land was needed. However, it also kept poor people away from the eyes of the more "genteel" townsfolk.

Today, with exception of some subsidized insitutions in Halifax, most of our social housing is outside of towns, some quite a distance. Farming is no longer a justification for locating social housing in isolated places where services, grocery stores and transportation are not available. To own, run and maintain a car is prohibitive to people in poverty. Social housing may cost the person less in rent, but they do not save any money if they are on social assistance as that amount is clawed back from them. Social housing which is located outside of towns tends to be very isolating for the people living in it, just like the poor houses were isolating to the people living in those. Social housing tends to lump all poor people into one area, whether it is a duplex, an apartment building or a neighbourhood, and it becomes another more contemporary form of a poor house.

It is still believed that middle class standards are achievable for everyone. Getting anything done to these standards requires a lot more work of poor people as they do not have the financial resources to purchase the tools (such as vehicles, insurance and gasoline, work clothes, equipment and such) to achieve those standards. Yet, poor people are shamed and shunned for this inability to fit in with the middle class. Every day someone on the internet posts a meme that shames and blames poor people and people on social assistance, equating them with crimes (poor people are on drugs, poor people steal) and laziness (people on welfare should just get a job).

Work and employment are still seen as the panacea for poverty. People in poverty are some of the hardest workers you will ever meet. Living in poverty is exhausting and requires a lot of work and resourcefulness on the part of the poor person. However, this is not recognized as work unless the poor person is paid for it. People who are not in poverty prefer to cast a cursory glance at a poor person and immediately label them as "lazy", without recognizing the work required of a person in poverty. The people in power say, "We will put you in paid employment and that will cure all the problems of your poverty." In many cases, this adds to the problems of a poor person by presenting them with the challenges of getting to work, of purchasing work clothing and often, childcare or eldercare. In the poor houses, people were set to work gardening, farming, picking oakum, housekeeping and caring for others in the poor house hospital. Although the poor house was not a great place to live, both physically or mentally, at least the workers' accommodations and meals were paid for. Today, thousands of workers (particularly women) are paid a minimum wage that is less than 50% of what is needed for the basics of living in Nova Scotia and are expected to pay for a mortgage or rent, food, electricity, clothing, childcare, and with today's education system, at least a computer with internet access and transportation. In no manner or form am I advocating for the return of poor houses. However, at least the people in the poor houses were fed, sheltered and clothed. Many poor persons today in Nova Scotia cannot achieve those basic human rights.

Today's poor are still buried in unmarked graves. Those in poverty who cannot afford funerals for their loved ones can apply to the provincial Employment Support and Income Assistance for financial support to bury their family members. If they qualify, the province will only supply a maximum of $3,800 plus some mileage for the cost of the funeral.[320] With funerals averaging an expense of $10,500, that means there will be no headstone to mark the burial spot of the poor.[321] Working class people also have a difficult time affording a funeral. Recently I was told the story of a working family whose family member had died. The family could not afford a burial for him. Instead, they had him cremated, put his ashes in his favourite shoes, snuck into the graveyard at night and dug a hole in which they buried the man's ashes in his shoes, close to other family graves.

There is a whole industry of decently paid people who have careers based on the regulation of the poor in Nova Scotia. Farmers, fishers and business people used to purchase paupers at auctions to work for their keep, making a profit off the poor. Now we have social workers, case workers, outreach workers, cabinet ministers and administrators in government departments making a well paid living from "treating" the poor while the poor remain poor. Their reluctance to end poverty is explained in that ending poverty would put an end to this well paid industry.

Refusal to accept employment, with a reason that is considered unreasonable in the unilateral opinion of the caseworker, results in termination of social assistance benefits to the poor person. The job may be dangerous to the physical or mental health of the poor person, or transportation, particularly in rural areas, may be a huge barrier to employment and training for a poor person. But their benefits will still be terminated. Affordable and accessible childcare is another barrier to employment that many poor people face. Just as an inmate would be denied access to a poor house or evicted from a poor house for refusing to work, so are our poor people denied access to monies that do not even cover their basic needs.

The fact that the Old Burying Ground on the corner of Barrington and Spring Garden Road in Halifax still receives federal funding to restore its headstones while the Poor House cemetery across the road on Spring Garden lies unmarked and unacknowledged by local and provincial governments tells us that the wealthy, even when dead, still get the taxpayers' dollars while the poor still do without.

Provincial legislation turns our social assistance system into its own "wholesome horror" by making life on social assistance as miserable as possible. Social assistance recipients are required to disclose extremely personal details about their lives and are expected to live on monies that are not nearly enough to meet their basic needs. They are often made to jump through many hoops – including "training," "workshops" and "education", while not recognizing or adequately funding childcare, transportation or eldercare, amongst other needs, and are cut off from benefits without warning or explanation.

We are still led to believe that addiction is a choice. Poor people often "self-medicate" with alcohol, cigarettes and other drugs (legal and illegal) to escape the constant anxiety, shame and pressures of poverty. They are censured for developing an addiction to the self-medication that helps them deal with the mental/physical pain of poverty. Just like the paupers who would be refused admittance into the poor house because they were addicted to alcohol, we are still refusing to recognize the needs of people under an immense amount of pressure when living in poverty. Instead of recognizing what people in poverty are dealing with, our culture blames them.

A book in itself could be written about how we are still carrying old fashioned attitudes towards people in poverty while refusing to look at the causes of their poverty. What is the answer to end these abusive attitudes and policies toward people in poverty? Some people advocate for a Basic Income or a Guaranteed Income.

A Basic Income, also called a Guaranteed Income, is an annual income for all citizens of the country. A country as wealthy as Canada would be able to afford it. A Basic Income program would give everyone enough income to afford the basic human rights of shelter, food, education and health care. Some people argue that the country cannot afford it. We can, however, if our goverrnments eliminate off-shore accounts for those who are wealthy enough to move their assets to a country outside of Canada, where they do not have to pay taxes. That is tax evasion and it hurts all citizens of Canada who work hard to make the country operate in fairness and equality. If big corporations, monopolies and banks were made to pay their fair share in taxes it would ensure a basic income for everyone and a much fairer share of the wealth that so many Canadians work to achieve. Instead of the wealth going to only a small group of people (the 1%), everyone would get their share of the wealth and it would eliminate poverty. Those who are wealthy could still be wealthy, but they would not be putting people in poverty so that they could be 'super rich'.

The advocates for these programs are up against a huge adversary called Wealth. Those who have wealth, those who pretend they have wealth, those who have been brainwashed into thinking wealth is what they want and deserve – all rely upon the poverty pay of other people, not just in this province but around the world, to make them wealthy. The products and the services that poor people make for the wealthier must be re-valued. The industries that have been built upon the regulation of poor people must be re-examined. Keeping people in poverty is a global dependency – i.e, the poor must be paid as little as possible to make the products and perform the services that make the owners rich. Even the middle classes depend upon the subjugation of the global poor. As a result, poor people today still live like the paupers of the past – in the shadows. Arthur Young, political observer and author of *The Farmers' Almanac and Calendar*, summed it up in 1771 when he wrote: "Everyone but an idiot knows that the lower classes must be kept poor, or they will never be industrious."[322]

As Judge Fetch of Halifax wrote in a letter of 1801:

Recently, the Grand Jury petitioned the Provincial Assembly for additional funds to support the poor. They proudly point to the Poor House brimming with paupers, orphans, and lunatics; yet complain that there are still those who beg in the streets, sleep in the doorways, and live in alleys. *When will they learn that they cannot sweep the town clean of miscreants until they change the circumstances that make men* (and women and children) *poor?*[323] (emphasis mine)

Arcadia Poor Farm Cemetery. Photo by author, May 2017.

Bibliography

Advertiser, Kentville newspaper "Efforts underway to preserve poor farm cemetery" August 31, 2001 Reporter- Brent Fox

Alchin, Linda K. "The Elizabethan Era – The Poor Law" www.elizabethan-era.org.uk. 2012

Armstrong, Peggy "Pages from the Past" *Valley Mirror* newspaper 1978

Atkins, T.B. *History of Halifax City* 2nd ed., Mika 1973

Bayside Home website "About Us" www.baysidehome.ca/About-Bay-Side-Home.html

Black History Canada www.blackhistorycanada.ca/events

Cahill, Bette L. *Butterbox Babies; Baby Sales Baby Deaths – New Revelations 15 Years Later* Fernwood Publishing, Halifax 2006

CBC News Nova Scotia November 27, 2010 "Fire at rehab centre contained" Reporter – Derek Kennedy

CBC News Nova Scotia May 27, 2016 "Trailer Park Boys' former set, Halifax County Rehab Centre lands to be Redeveloped" Reporter – Lisa Blackburn

Chronicle Herald, newspaper "Historic Cemetery gets federal cash for restoration" December 20, 2011

Chronicle Herald newspaper "Cole Harbour Rehab Centre to be turned into parkland" May 24, 2016

Coast, newspaper "The Unclaimed dead beneath our City's Streets; Thousands lay buried under Spring Garden Road' October 29, 2015 Reporter – Maura Donovan

Desroches, Cheryl, "For Them but Never Really Theirs: Finding a Place for the 'Aged' Within State-Funded Institutions in Nineteenth-Century Nova Scotia" in *Journal of Canadian Historical Association Canada* Vol. 20 No. 1 2009

Diagel, Jean "Acadia 1604-1763: An Historical Synthesis" in The Acadians of the Maritimes; Thematic Studies Centre de etudes acadiennes Universite de Moncton, 1982

Dickens, Charles, *Oliver Twist* 1837

Digby Courier Newspaper, January 9, 1885

Digby Courier Newspaper, Interview with Edward Robicheau March 6, 1989

Disraeli, Benjamin, M.P. *Sybil* 1845

Eaton, A.W.H. *The History of the County of Kings* Salem Press Company 1910

Foster, Malcolm Cecil *An Annapolis Valley Saga* 1992

Francis, Daniel "The Development of the Lunatic Asylum in the Maritime Provinces" *Acadiensis* 1977

George, Philip "Picking Junk and Oakum: How your Workhouse and Criminal Ancestors picked Oakum" www.HistoryHouse.co.uk./articles/junk_and_oakum.html 2016

Hattie, W.H. Dr., Report on Public Charities 1921

Holmes Whitehead, Ruth *Black Loyalists: Southern Settlers of Nova Scotia's First Free Black Community* Nimbus Publishing, Halifax NS 2013

Horton Poor Farm – Burial Grounds Society www.burialgroundscaresociety. wordpress.com/horton-poor-farm-cemetery/

Kendrix, Jennifer E.K. "Punishing the Poor Through Welfare Reform; Cruel and Unusual?" in *Duke Law Journal Online* March 2015

Key dates in the Sociological history and development of Great Britain 1300-1899 PDF www.thepotteries.org/dates/poor/htm

Kroll, Robert E., *Intimate Fragments: An Irreverent Chronicle of Early Halifax* Nimbus Publishing Ltd., Halifax 1985

Laffoley, Steven, *The Halifax Poor House Fire: A Victorian Tragedy* Pottersfield Press, Lawrencetown Beach, Nova Scotia 2016

Lawson, J.M. "Yarmouth Past and Present" *Yarmouth Herald* newspaper 1902

Marble, Dr. Allan E. *Physicians, Pestilence, and the Poor: A History of Medicine and Social Conditions in Nova Scotia 1800-1867* Trafford Publishing, Victoria BC 2006

Marble, Dr. Allan E. *Surgeons Smallpox and the Poor: A History of Medicine and Social Conditions in Nova Scotia 1749-1799.* McGill Queen's 1993

Morning Herald (Halifax) 1884-1885

Maclean's Magazine (Brian Bethune) "How a Volcanic Eruption made 1816 the Year Without Summer" March 12, 2013

Morton, Suzanne "Old Women and Their Place 1881-1931" *Atlantis*, Vol. 20 No. 1 1995

Municipality of the County of Annapolis – *Old Houses of Annapolis County* MFN 43-02-00662

Ottawa Free Press, April 4, 1885

Page, Dr. A.C. Report on Public Charities, various years

PANS RG 35-102 List of Paupers in the Poor House at Halifax 1802-1811

PANS Mi'kmaq Holdings Resource Guide Volume XIX Part 4 Appendix N. 24 and Annual Reports MG15 Vol. 3 No. 76

Paul, Daniel N. *We Were Not the Savages: Collision between European and Native American Civilizations* 3rd Edition Fernwood Publishing, Halifax, NS 2008

Perry, Hattie, *This was Barrington* Published by the Nova Scotia Museum 1973

Poor of Digby (The) An Enquiry 1885

Raddall, T.H. *Warden of the North* Halifax, Nimbus Publishing 1993

Reed, Gus "Halifax County Poor Farm – Bissett Road in Cole Harbour Parks and Trails Association" June 9, 2008 http://www.chpta.org/2008/06/halifax-county-poors-farm-bissett-road.html

Reports on Public Charities, Nova Scotia Legislature House of Assembly Journals Years 1889-1957

Riverview Enhanced Living: Our History www.ourriverview.com/our-history.html

Roth, Rev. D. Luther *Acadia and the Acadians* Lutheran Publication Society, Philadelphia 1890

Rhude, Steven srhude@blogspot.ca

Senior Scribes *Poverty Poor Houses and Private Philanthropy*, A New Horizon Project, Health Promotion and Programs Branch, Health Canada, Communications Nova Scotia 1996

Shaping a community – Black Refugees in Nova Scotia www.pier21.ca/research/immigration-history/shaping-a-community-black-refugees-in-nova-scotia

Simpson, Cynthia "The treatment of Halifax's poor house dead during the nineteenth and twentieth centuries" Unpublished Thesis St. Mary's University, Halifax 2011

Sinclair, G.L. Dr. Report on Public Charities, various years

Spring Hill Heritage Group, "Heritage Corner" September 13, 2006 http://www.springhillheritage.ca/Springhill_Heritage_Group/HC-13sept2006.html

Statutes (the) at Large Passed in the Several General Assemblies Held in His Majesty's Province of Nova Scotia, held the first day of August, Anno Domini 1759

Thompson, Brenda & Moore, Barbara "Please Don't Bury Me: Women's Response to the CHST" Transition House Association of Nova Scotia 1995

Wagstaff, Margaret "The Colchester County Home" at the Historeum Blog July 11, 2013 WEBSITE

Waterville County Poor Farm – Burial Grounds Care Society www.freewebs.com/burialcare/watervillepoor.htm

Watson, T.D. "The Slave in Canada," presented at the Nova Scotia Historical Society March 18, 1898

Windsor, The Town of, *Gateway to the Valley* A Centennial Publication of the Town of Windsor, 1977

Wolfville Acadian newspaper, December 1922

Woolaver, Lance "Maud Lewis; The Heart on the Door" Spencer Books 2016

Woolaver, Lance "The Poor Farm" play, 1999

Young, Arthur "The Farmers' Calendar" 1771" London, UK

Endnotes

1   Sources for the Study of the Poor Law in Sheffield, Sheffield City Council v.1.2 Apr. 2013 p.5

2   Henry VIII had Anne Boleyn beheaded after three years of marriage and promptly married Jane Seymour.

3   Ibid p.5

4   Ibid p.6

5   Linda K. Alchin, "The Elizabethan Era-The Poor Law" <www.elizabeth-an-era.org.uk>

6   Key dates in the sociological history and development of Great Britain 1300-1899 PDF <thepotteries.org/dates/poor.htm>

7   ibid

8   Alchin, "The Elizabethan Era"

9   ibid

10   ibid

11   ibid

12   ibid

13   ibid

14   Senior Scribes, *Poverty Poor Houses and Private Philanthropy,* A New Horizon Project, Health Promotion and Programs Branch, Health Canada, Communications Nova Scotia 1996p.15

15   Jennifer E.K. Kendrex, "Punishing the Poor Through Welfare Reform; Cruel and Unusual?" in Duke Law Journal Online, March 2015 p.130. The rich could be idle, and it was not seen as a "sin" as they had wealth to support their idleness.

16   Ibid

17   Ibid p.130

18   Philip George, "Picking June and Oakum: How your Workhouse and Criminal Ancestors picked Oakum" <HistoryHouse.co.uk/articles/junk_and_oakum.html> 2016

19   Senior Scribes p.19

20   Judith Fingard, "The Relief of the Unemployed Poor in Saint John, Halifax and St. John's, 1815-1860," *Acadiensis* 1975 p.39

21 Charles Dickens, "Oliver Twist," 1837, Benjamin Disraeli, M.P. "Sybil" 1845

22 The Statutes at Large Passed in the Several General Assemblies Held in His Majesty's Province of Nova Scotia, held the first day of August, Anno Domini 1759 p.41

23 Ibid p.42

24 A.W.H. Eaton, *The History of the County of Kings*, The Salem Press Company, 1910

25 Daniel N. Paul, "Mi'kmaq Social Values and Economy," in *We Were Not the Savages*, 3rd Edition, Fernwood Publishing, Halifax, July 2008, p.39

26 Jean Daigle, *Acadia 1604–1763: An Historical Synthesis in the Acadians of the Maritimes*, Thematic Studies Centre de etudes acadiennes, Universite de Moncton, 1982 p.17

27 Paul, *We Were Not*, p.9

28 Dr. Allan E. Marble, *Surgeons Smallpox and the Poor: A History of Medicine and Social Conditions in Nova Scotia 1749-1799* McGill Queen's 1993 p.68

29 *The Poor of Digby: Official Enquiry* – Memorial Asking for Enquiry – Letter signed by E.R. Oakes, John S. McNeill, and Henry M. Robichau, Halifax April 22, 1885. Newspaper reports were as follows: *Morning Herald*, December 1884, February 10, 12, 27, and March 4 1885; *Digby Courier*, January 9, 1885; *Ottawa Free Press*, April 4, 1885

30 Legislature of Nova Scotia, Session 1886 *The Poor of Digby Official Enquiry* 29 April 1885, p.4

31 The Poor of Digby: Official Enquiry — Memorial Asking for Enquiry — Letter signed by E.R. Oakes, John S. McNeill, and Henry M. Robichau, Halifax, April 22, 1885.

32 Bell, F.H. Commissioners Report in The Poor of Digby: Official Enquiry 1885 P. 5

33 Bell, F.H. Commissioners Report in The Poor of Digby 1885 P. 13.

34 Ibid p.14

35 Ibid p.37

36 Malcolm Cecil Foster, *An Annapolis Valley Saga* p.89-90

37 The Poor of Digby p.14

38 The Poor of Digby p.16

39 Senior Scribes p.100

40 Senior Scribes p.18
41 Marble, Allan E p.363 footnote 104
42 Municipality of the County of Annapolis Old Houses of Annapolis County MFN 43-02-00662
43 Senior Scribes, p.151
44 Ibid. p.152
45 Senior Scribes p.74
46 J.M. Lawson, *Yarmouth Past and Present*. Yarmouth Herald, 1902 p.591–92
47 Senior Scribes, p.71
48 Peggy Armstrong, "Pages from the Past" *Valley Mirror* newspaper 1978. The collection of articles published in this paper are compiled in a file at the Annapolis Valley Regional Library.
49 Marble, *Physicians*, p.363 footnote 104
50 Senior Scribes p.146
51 Ibid p.149
52 Marble, *Physicians*, p.362
53 Senior Scribes, Chapter 3 Page 71
54 ibid
55 Marble, *Physicians*, p.363
56 ibid
57 ibid
58 Marble, *Physicians*, p.363
59 Ibid p.364
60 The Poor of Digby p.16
61 Page, Report on Public Charities 1889 p.8; Sinclair, Report on Public Charities 1899 p.28
62 Page, Report on Public Charities 1889 p.8
63 Sinclair, Report on Public Charities 1890 p.7
64 Senior Scribes p.72
65 ibid
66 Senior Scribes p.73,75
67 Dr. A.C. Page, Report on Public Charities, 1889 p.11
68 Ibid 1890 p.5
69 Ibid 1891 p.7
70 Senior Scribes p.80, 76

71   ibid

72   Senior Scribes p.158

73   Page, Report on Public Charities 1889 p.6

74   Ibid 1890 p.7

75   Ibid 1891 p.13

76   Ibid 1892 p.10

77   Ibid 1898 p.11

78   Sinclair, Report on Public Charities 1899 p.1899

79   Senior Scribes p.158

80   Sinclair, Report on Public Charities 1904 p.41,42

81   Senior Scribes p.82

82   Senior Scribes p.133

83   Page, Report on Public Charities 1891 p.11-12

84   Ibid 1892 p.8

85   Ibid 1989 p.7

86   Sinclair, Report on Public Charities 1899 p.27-28

87   Senior Scribes p.83

88   Page, Report on Public Charities 1891 p.14

89   Senior Scribes, p.85

90   Perry, Hattie p.73

91   Page, A.C. Dr. Report on Public Charities 1891 p. 11

92   Page, A.C. Dr. Report on Public Charities 1892 p. 8 Dr. Page is refer-
     ring to Matthew 23:27 of the Bible in which a Whitened Sepulchre is a
     white washed tomb full of "bones of the dead and the unclean."

93   ibid

94   Senior Scribes p. 13

95   Senior Scribes p.87, footnote 50

96   Senior Scribes p.86

97   Page, Report on Public Charities 1890 p.49

98   Ibid p.4

99   ibid

100 Page, Report on Charities 1891 p.6

101 Senior Scribes p.87

102 Senior Scribes p.88 footnote 54

103 Senior Scribes p.88–9

104 Senior Scribes p.89-90

105 Report of Humane Conditions, Journals of the House of Assembly 1923 p.15

106 Ibid 1928 p.18

107 Senior Scribes p.90–91

108 Senior Scribes p.94

109 Senior Scribes p.95

110 Ibid pg.96

111 Margaret Wagstaff, The Colchester County Home in At the Historeum Blog, July 11, 2013

112 Senior Scribes p.96

113 Senior Scribes, p.119

114 Page, Report on Public Charities 1890 p.9

115 Page, Report on Public Charities 1892 p.12

116 Page, Report on Public Charities 1890 p.9

117 Ibid 1891 p.9

118 Sinclair, Report on Public Charities 1899 p.34

119 Senior Scribes p.119

120 Gus Reed, "Halifax County Poor Farm," blog post, Bissett Road–Cole Harbour Parks and Trails Association, June 9, 2008, <www.chpta. org/2008/06/halifax-county-poors-farm-bissett-road.html>

121 Senior Scribes p.119

122 Ibid p.120

123 ibid

124 Lisa Blackburn, "Trailer Park Boys' former set, Halifax County Rehab Centre lands to be Redeveloped," CBC News May 27, 2016

125 Derek Kennedy, "Fire at former rehab centre contained," CBC News November 27, 2010

126 "Cole Harbour Rehab Centre to be turned into parkland," Chronicle Herald
May 24, 2016

127 Senior Scribes p.97

128 Senior Scribes p.97

129 Ibid p.92–98

130 Ibid p.99

131 Sinclair, Report on Public Charities 1899, p.43–44

132 Pat Crowe, Springhill Heritage Group, "Heritage Corner," Springhill

161 Senior Scribes p.132

162 Senior Scribes, p.137, footnote 265

163 ibid

164 Page, Report on Public Charities 1889 p.6

165 Ibid 1890 p.8

166 Ibid 1891 p.12

167 Ibid 1898 p.13

168 Ibid 1899 p.37

169 Senior Scribes p.140

170 Ibid p.141

171 Riverview Enhanced Living; Our History <www.ourriverview.com/our-history.html>

172 Page, Report on Public Charities 1890, p.5

173 Page, Report on Public Charities 1891 p.6

174 Ibid 1898 p.17

175 Sinclair, Report on Charities 1899 p.51

176 Senior Scribes p.129-130 footnote #232

177 Senior Scribes p.130 footnote 233

178 Ibid p.131

179 Ibid p.133

180 Senior Scribes p.91

181 Ibid p.92, footnote 71

182 Ibid p.92

183 ibid

184 Page, Report on Public Charities 1898 p.18

185 Ibid 1899 p.60-61

186 Senior Scribes p.142, footnotes 278, 279

187 Senior Scribes p.142–44

188 Riverview Home Corporation – Our History http://riverviewhome.ca/history

189 Page, Report on Public Charities p.5-6

190 Ibid 1891 p.8

191 Ibid 1892 p.3

192 Ibid 1898 p.15

193 Senior Scribes p.145–46

194 Riverview Home Corporation <riverviewhome.ca>

Record September 13, 2006 <www.springhillheritage.ca/Springhill_
Heritage_Group/HC-13sept2006.html>

133 Senior Scribes p.100

134 Page, Report on Charities 1892 p.11

135 Sinclair, , Report on Public Charities 1899 p.33

136 Environmental Assessment Registration: Highway 101 Digby to
Marshalltown Corridor February 2017 Prepared by Stantec Consulting
Ltd., Dartmouth NS Project No. 121414143 Section 5.6 p176

137 Senior Scribes p.111

138 Marble, *Surgeons*, p.32

139 Ibid See Marble's Chapter One – Arrival, Settlement, and Health Care

140 Marble, *Surgeons*, p.80

141 Ibid p.83

142 Senior Scribes p.113

143 Ibid p.114

144 Senior Scribes p.115 footnote 169

145 Laffoley, Steven *The Halifax Poor House Fire: A Victorian Tragedy*,
Pottersfield Press 2016. This book examines the enquiry into this fire;
how it happened, why it spread, why so many perished.

146 Page, Report on Public Charities 1890 p.9

147 Senior Scribes p.115

148 Senior Scribes p.116

149 Senior Scribes p.120

150 Page, Report on Public Charities 1896 p.18

151 Ibid 1898 p.6

152 Senior Scribes p.121

153 ibid

154 Senior Scribes p.132

155 Page, Report on Public Charities 1891 p.10, 11

156 Page, Report on Public Charities 1892, p.7

157 Page, Report on Public Charities 1893

158 "Horton Poor Farm," Burial Grounds Care Society <https://burial-
groundscaresociety.wordpress.com/horton-poor-farm-cemetery>

159 Sinclair, Report on Public Charities 1899 p.26

160 Burial Grounds Care Society <www.freewebs.com/burialcare/horton-
poorfarmcemeter.htm>

195 Senior Scribes p.146
196 Page, Report on Public Charities 1898 p.17
197 Sinclair, Report on Public Charities, 1899 p.43
198 Senior Scribes p.147
199 Senior Scribes p.148–49
200 Page, Report on Public Charities 1898 p.13
201 Sinclair, Report on Public Charities 1899 p.38–39
202 Senior Scribes p.149
203 Sinclair, Report on Public Charities 1899 p.39
204 Senior Scribes p.149-150
205 Senior Scribes p.150
206 Sinclair, Report on Public Charities 1913 p.32
207 Dr. W.H. Hattie, Report on Public Charities 19214 p.17
208 Senior Scribes p.150--51
209 Senior Scribes p.152, footnotes 333, 337
210 ibid, footnote 337
211 Page, Report on Public Charities 1889 p.7
212 Ibid 1890 p.6
213 Ibid 1898 p.12
214 Sinclair, Report on Public Charities 1899 p.35–6
215 Senior Scribes p.153 and footnote#340
216 Page, Report on Public Charities 1896 p.15
217 Ibid 1897 p.18
218 Ibid 1898 p.18
219 Sinclair, Report on Public Charities 1899 p.50
220 Ibid 1902 p.38,39
221 Page, Report on Public Charities 1898 p.20–1
222 Ibid 1900 p.38-39
223 Senior Scribes p.156
224 Senior Scribes p.133
225 Burial Grounds Care Society: Waterville County Poor Farm
    http://www.freewebs.com/burialcare/watervillecountypoor.htm
226 The Wolfville Acadian newspaper, supplement to the Kentville Advertiser,
    December 1922
227 Senior Scribes p.124
228 Page, Report on Public Charities 1888 p.9-10

229 Page, Report on Public Charities 1892 p.6

230 Sinclair, Report on Public Charities 1892 p.23

231 *Gateway to the Valley* (A Centennial Publication of the Town of Windsor) 1977 p.96

232 Senior Scribes p.127

233 T.D. Watson, "The Slave in Canada," presentation at the Nova Scotia Historical Society, March 18, 1898, p.2

234 Black History Canada – Mathieu DeCosta http://www.blackhistorycanada.ca/events.php?themeid=21&id=1

235 Ibid p.3

236 Ibid p.5

237 ibid

238 Black History Canada – the Black Loyalists http://www.blackhistorycanada.ca/

239 Shaping a Community – Black Refugees in Nova Scotia —<www.pier21.ca/research/immigration-history/shaping-a-community-black-refugees-in-nova-scotia-0>

240 Ruth Whitehead Holmes, "Black Loyalists: Southern Settlers of Nova Scotia's First Free Black Communities" 2013 p.161

241 Senior Scribes 1996 p.152

242 Marble, *Physicians*, p.315

243 Ibid p.315–16

244 Ibid

245 Marble, *Physicians*, p.196–97, footnotes 22, 25

246 Maclean's Magazine, March 12, 2013

247 Marble, *Physicians*, p.319

248 Ibid 319-320

249 ibid

250 Whitehead Holmes, *Black Loyalists* p.165

251 Ibid p.321

252 Ibid p.322–23

253 Page, Report on Public Charities 1881

254 Sinclair, Report on Public Charities 1899 p.32

255 Steven Laffoley, *The Halifax Poor House Fire: A Victorian Tragedy*, Pottersfield Press, 2016

256 Rev. D. Luther, Roth, "Acadia and the Acadians" Lutheran Publication Press 1890 p.53

257 Marble, *Physicians*, p.302–03

258 Ibid

259 PANS RG35-102 List of Paupers in the Poor House at Halifax 1802-1811

260 Marble, *Physicians*, p. 301

261 Paul, *We Were Not*, Chapter 10 "Dispossession and the Imposition of Poverty"

262 PANS Mi'kmaq Holdings Resource Guide Volume XIX Part 4 Appendix N. 24

263 PANS Mi'kmaq Holdings Resource Guide, annual reports MG 15 Vol. 3 No. 76

264 Paul, *We Were Not*, p.193. I highly recommend this book for a comprehensive understanding of what the Mi'kmaq of Nova Scotia endured after colonization.

265 Page, Report on Public Charities 1890 p.6 1891, p.13

266 The Poor of Digby Enquiry 1885 p.11

267 ibid

268 Cheryl Desroches, "For Them but Never Really Theirs: Finding a Place for the 'Aged' within State-Funded Institutions in Nineteenth-Century Nova Scotia," *Journal of Canadian Historical Association Canada* Vol. 20, No. 1 (2009), p.74

269 Desroches, p.63

270 Desroches, p.60

271 Desroches, p.59

272 Sinclair, Report on Public Charities 1899 p.34

273 Daniel Francis, "The Development of the Lunatic Asylum in the Maritime Provinces," *Acadiensis* 1977 p.28

274 Senior Scribes p.108–09

275 Bette L Cahill, *Butterbox Babies; Baby Sales Baby Deaths – New Revelations 15 Years Later* Fernwood Publishing, Halifax 2006

276 Laffoley, *The Halifax Poor House Fire*

277 Suzanne Morton, "Old Women and Their Place 1881-1931" *Atlantis*, Vol. 20, No. 1 1995 p.25

278 Verse on a tombstone in Devon, England

279 *Digby Courier*, March 6 1985 on microfiche, the Digby Library

280 Cynthia Simpson, "The treatment of Halifax's poor house dead during the nineteenth and twentieth centuries," unpublished thesis, St. Mary's University August 2011 p.47-48

281 Simpson, "The treatment" p.77

282 Moira Donovan, "The Unclaimed dead beneath our City's Streets; Thousands lay buried under Spring Garden Road," *The Coast*, Halifax, NS October 29, 2015

283 Marble, Allan E. *Physicians* p.217

284 Ibid p.68

285 Ibid p.68, 82, 71

286 Robert E. Kroll (ed) *Intimate Fragments: An Irreverent Chronicle of Early Halifax* Nimbus 1985 p.74-75

287 Simpson, "The Treatment," p.81

288 T.B. Atkins, *History of Halifax City* 2nd ed., Mika, 1973 p.201

289 T.H. Raddall, *Warden of the North*, Halifax, Nimbus 1993 p.55

290 Simpson, "The Treatment" p.73

291 Ibid p.82

292 Kroll, *Intimate Fragments*, p.52

293 "Historic Halifax Cemetery gets federal cash for restoration," *Chronicle Herald*, December 20, 2011

294 Woolaver, Lance "Maud Lewis:The Heart on the Door" Spencer Books, Halifax, 2016 p. 294

295 ibid

296 Ibid p. 295

297 Senior Scribes, "Poverty, Poor Houses and Private Philanthropy" Province of Nova Scotia 1996 p. 93

298 Woolaver, Lance "Maud Lewis:The Heart on the Door" Spencer Books, Halifax, 2016 p. 294

299 Acadian Recorder October 30, 1819

300 Acadian Recorder November 6, 1819

301 Acadian Recorder November 27, 1819

302 See "A Nova Scotia Poor house: A View from the Inside" by Richard Wagner, Senior Scribes p. 165-174

303 Woolaver, Lance "Maud Lewis; The Heart on the Door" Spencer Books, Halifax, 2016 p. 148-155

304 ibid

306 Woolaver, Lance "Maud Lewis; The Heart on the Door" p. 154

307 Senior Scribes p. 84

308 Ibid p. 108

309 Defoe, Daniel "Roxana: or, the Fortunate Mistress. Being a History of the Life and Vast Variety of Fortunes of Mademoiselle de Beleau"London, 1742

310 Woolaver, Lance "The Poor Farm" 1999

311 Laffoley, Steven "The Halifax Poor House Fire: A Victorian Tragedy" Pottersfield Press, Lawrencetown NS 2016

312 Senior Scribes p. 109

313 Woolaver, Lance "The Heart on the Door" p. 154

314 Senior Scribes p. 84

315 Ibid p. 108

316 Defoe, Daniel "Roxana: or, the Fortunate Mistress. Being a History of the Life and Vast Variety of Fortunes of Mademoiselle de Beleau"London, 1742

317 Laffoley p. 154-155

318 Sinclair, G.L. Dr. Report on Public Charities 1899 p. 41

319 Thompson, Brenda & Moore, Barbara "Please Don't Bury Me: Nova Scotia Women's Response to the CHST" 1995

320 https://novascotia.ca/coms/employment/documents/ESIA_Manual/ESIA_Policy_Manual.pdf

321 John DeMont, "It costs a lot to die in Nova Scotia," *Chronicle Herald* Sept.5, 2012

322 Young, Arthur, The Farmers'Calendar 1771

323 Kroll, Robert E. "Intimate Fragments" p.75

Index

145

About the Author

Photo by Gary Fraser.

Brenda Thompson has been an anti-poverty activist and writer for more than 30 years. She holds a BA in Women's Studies from MSVU and a masters degree in Sociology from Acadia University. As a former 'welfare mother' and lifetime low wage earner, she has lived with poverty issues firsthand. Her first book, *The Single Mothers' Survival Guide for Nova Scotia* is in its 6th edition. Recipient of a Leadership Award from the Atlantic Centre of Excellence in Women's Health, Brenda was also the subject of several national news and documentary stories during the 1980s and 1990s. Brenda is a past vice-president of the national Ottawa-based organization Canada Without Poverty. Living in the Annapolis Royal area for more than 20 years, she has discovered her passion for local history. This book is a combination of both of Brenda's passions. Brenda lives with her husband, daughters and parents in the beautiful and historic Annapolis Royal area of Nova Scotia.